FORGED BY THE FIRE

A Mother's Journey Through Grief,
Faith and Finding Purpose

DEBORAH SIMPSON

Forged by the Fire

Copyright © 2025 Deborah Simpson

All rights reserved. No part of this publication may be reproduced, distributed, or transmitted in any form or by any means, including photocopying, recording, or other electronic or mechanical methods, without the prior written permission of the copyright owner, except in the case of brief quotations used in reviews, critical articles, or other non-commercial uses permitted by copyright law.

This is a work of nonfiction. Names, characters, places, and incidents are drawn from the author's life and research. Any resemblance to actual events or persons, living or dead, is purely coincidental unless otherwise noted.

For information, permissions, or bulk orders, contact:

Email: deborah@celebrateandinspirelife.com

Website: www.celebrateandinspirelife.com

First Edition: November 2025

Printed in the United States of America

This book is dedicated to my three children, Alayna Joy, Katelyn Elizabeth, and Jonathan Taylor. It has been my greatest gift to be your mother. May you know how much I love you, for all of your days.

CONTENTS

FOREWORD

INTRODUCTION

PART I JOURNEY THROUGH THE WORST DAY

    CHAPTER 1   THE BEST FAMILY WEEKEND 1

    CHAPTER 2   THE CALM BEFORE THE STORM 7

    CHAPTER 3   THE SADDEST DARKEST DAY 13

    CHAPTER 4   THE GATHERING OF OUR BROKEN HEARTS 25

    CHAPTER 5   THE CELEBRATION + BURIAL 33

PART II JOURNEY THROUGH GRIEF

    CHAPTER 6   THE FIRST YEAR - 2020 49

    CHAPTER 7   THE SECOND YEAR - 2021 101

    CHAPTER 8   THE THIRD YEAR - 2022 119

    CHAPTER 9   THE FOURTH AND FIFTH YEAR - 2023 + 2024 141

PART III JOURNEY TO HEALING

    CHAPTER 10   THE GRACE OF LAMENT 157

    CHAPTER 11   SOUL CARE 163

    CHAPTER 12   FAMILY 183

    CHAPTER 13   LOGISTICS 199

CLOSING LETTER 209

ACKNOWLEDGMENTS 213

ABOUT THE AUTHOR 219

FOREWORD

The Lord led me to write this, and I have prayed that it will be well with your soul for His glory. There are people God places in our lives for a time and a season, and then there are those He knits into the fabric of our hearts forever.

Debs is one of those souls in my life. We met when I first opened our pregnancy help medical clinic, where she volunteered with a heart full of love, passion, and compassion to serve moms who were experiencing an unplanned pregnancy. From the moment I met her, I knew she was special; she had God's heart of kindness, love, and compassion.

Then came the day I heard the devastating news that her precious son, Jonathan, had gone home to be with Jesus. A sharp pain pierced my heart; even though I knew he was dancing before the Lord, wrapped in His precious arms close to His heart, I could not understand how or why.

However, my more substantial pain was for Debs, for the unbearable sorrow of a mother who had to live without her baby boy. At Jonathan's celebration of life, I stood among so many others who shared the exact weight of grief, the same unspoken ache. Jonathan was deeply loved, and his absence left an emptiness that only God Himself could fill.

I remember seeing Debs and wanting to hold her, never to let her go. Yet, even in her suffering, she had so much strength that could only come from our Heavenly Father above. Her faith, unwavering and bold, stirred something deep within me.

Instead of flowers, the Simpsons asked friends and family to donate to Heartbeat of Miami in Jonathan's honor. Helping moms who are fac-

FOREWORD

ing an unplanned pregnancy and in crisis is very near and dear to Deb's heart, as she knows firsthand what that experience is like. She found herself with an unplanned pregnancy and an uncertain future with the father of her children when she was expecting her oldest daughter, Alayna.

Even in experiencing the grief of losing her son, Jonathan, she remained passionate about fighting for the life of every unborn child and the physical, spiritual, and mental well-being of their mother and the entire family.

This is a beautiful juxtaposition of knowing both the joy and sorrow of birthing and burying your child. Believing that the joy greatly outweighs the sorrow in this life; and that every mother and every child should experience pure love at first sight as you lock your eyes for the first time. It has been a privilege to partner with Debs in this cause and witness her healing as she channels her passion into purpose.

I watched her take refuge in the arms of the Most High, walking through the fire of her pain with a grace that inspired me and so many others. I prayed for her daily from a distance, lifting her as she faced each new challenge and sorrow with unshakable trust in the Lord.

Her testimony became a beacon of hope, not just for me but for many mothers who had experienced the unimaginable loss of a child. I was able to share her story with them. Through her pain, she ministered. Through her faith, she inspired. And through this book, she will continue to bring glory to God.

This book is more than just words on a page. It is a testimony of the hope of glory we have in Christ Jesus. The hope that one day, we will all be reunited with those we love. Where there will be no more tears, no more pain, only everlasting joy in His presence. May every reader find comfort, strength, and the assurance that even in our deepest sorrow, God is with us, and His promise of eternity is sure.

With love and in His grace,

Martha E. Avila

President and Co-Founder - Heartbeat of Miami Crisis Pregnancy Clinics

INTRODUCTION

I never wanted to be part of this club, and if you have picked up this book, then you most likely have joined the club that we wish we could pay to go back and revoke our membership from — the club of mothers who have lost a young child. It is the most intimate and personal loss imaginable. It has been compared to losing a limb, as your child is scientifically forever a part of your body, and we have to adapt to them missing for the rest of our lives.

I want you to know how sorry I am that you have experienced this heart-wrenching, soul-crushing loss. I pray that the Lord can use me as a metaphorical shoulder to cry on, the comfort of a warm hug, the refreshing shower to bring life back into your soul and wash away the despair, even just for a moment. I want to be the voice of a friend encouraging you, that you will be okay. You will rise above the waves of grief that often threaten to take you under. Through this life's journey with the Lord, you will be forged and refined by the fire, just as I have been and will continue to be.

You are in good company if you have begged the Lord to take this cup from you; I have too. Jesus also asked this of the Father when he was in the Garden of Gethsemane on his way to be crucified on the cross; he understood to the greatest extent the pain and agony of living in this broken world and enduring suffering. May we follow his example as he submitted and said, "Not my will, but yours be done." Luke 22:42

The Bible promises in Psalm 34:18, "The LORD is close to the brokenhearted and saves those who are crushed in spirit." and "But they

INTRODUCTION

who wait for the LORD shall renew their strength; they shall mount up with wings like eagles; they shall run and not be weary; they shall walk and not faint." Isaiah 40:31

I would have given almost anything to turn back time on Tuesday, February 11, 2020, when my son Jonathan left my arms on this earth and was welcomed into the arms of Jesus. Instead, almost instantly, the Lord gave me the tremendous gift of being able to pour out my every feeling, my every question, my every doubt, my every praise and encouragement, my every faith-filled cry, and my every moment of complete despair onto the notes section of my phone. Those notes would eventually become part of this book you are holding in your hands or listening to in your ears.

It would have been challenging to reflect years later and pinpoint all the twists and turns, valleys and mountain peaks that I have navigated as I journeyed through grief these past 5 years. Writing/journaling in that very moment has been a sweet salve of healing to my soul and so many others, as I shared with friends and family.

If you are in the midst of your journey through grief, you will have moments throughout this book to reflect on the very moment you are living, a chance to look back and release or remember, and an invitation to have hope again for the future. I pray that this process relieves some of the pressure that makes you feel like you want to explode; that you will be able to take a few deep breaths and rest in God's love, peace, and joy. You have permission to meet me wherever you are today.

The stages of grief can often be described as:

- Denial: How could this be happening? It must be a mistake; I must be dreaming; they aren't gone.

- Anger: How could a loving God allow this? This wasn't supposed to happen to me; I will never worship God again; this is the fault of someone or a stranger in your life.

- Bargaining: If I just do this, it will change the outcome. Instead, take me. If I am a better person, then this won't happen.

- Depression: Feeling tired, sad, or numb, overwhelmed with the requirements of daily life, experiencing despair and hopelessness, thinking others won't understand your loss, low energy.

- Acceptance: Seeking out new meaning, hope for the future, feeling more secure and relaxed, able to tolerate emotions and be vulnerable, taking care of yourself, and having self-compassion.

During this journey, you will quickly realize that you will go through these "stages" multiple times in all different cycles, sometimes on random days, other times on special occasions, and sometimes two stages simultaneously. That's natural and okay; you will see this displayed throughout my writing in this book. The important thing is that you don't get stuck in denial, anger, bargaining, or depression for too long. That is why I wrote this book. I am here to help the Lord bring you into healing and lead you into acceptance and hope, so you can thrive again.

As important as the journey of grief is, I also want to invite you into the grace of lament as Mark Vroegop refers to it in his book, Dark Clouds, Deep Mercy. He states, *"Lament invites us to grieve and trust, to struggle and believe. Lament is a prayer in pain that leads to trust."* Lament typically asks at least 2 questions that we don't usually think we are allowed to voice: *(1) "Where are you, God?" (2) "If you love me, why is this happening?"*

We will walk together and embrace the Lord's invitation to draw close to Him in this season, instead of resigning into silence. We will bring every complaint, request, and expression of trust and/or praise to Him.

One attribute of God's character that I held on to from that February 2020 morning and has sustained me, is that the loss and death of my son was never God's original plan; he never wanted me or you to suffer in this way. He wanted us to enjoy fellowship with him for all eternity, without pain or the tainting of sin that we experience in this world through death. And I am so thankful for His redemptive plan to use/redeem all things together for our good and His glory, if only we would believe in Him and accept His love. Romans 8:28

INTRODUCTION

So, what does this mean for us now? How do we navigate the winding roads of life and the cliffs on either side of us that threaten to topple us to our deaths? We must ground ourselves in the truths of God's word and prayer and surround ourselves with a community that will step in to handle or assist with planning, feeding, and cleaning, just sit in silence or shed a few (or a lot of) tears with us.

I often think about the passage in the Bible that talks about God leading Jesus into the wilderness; Jesus rebuked Satan with God's word when he tried to tempt him multiple times. When the devil tries to bring us down into despair, we will need to know in our heads and hearts what God says in John 16:33, "I have told you these things, so that in me you may have peace. In this world, you will have trouble. But take heart! I have overcome the world." We have assurance that we will not suffer in vain and that we will not suffer endlessly when we place our trust in God.

Today, I listened to a story of how a sword is forged in fire, and I could relate to the process. Swords are forged by heating metal until it's malleable, then hammering it into shape. This process involves heating and cooling the metal repeatedly. This increases the strength of the sword's steel, and the last step is to sharpen the blade.

The breathtaking artwork on my book cover is inspired by a painting gifted to me by my mother for my 40th birthday. She knew that I had been forged by the fire like the sword described above. Through this painting, she honored the journey I had traveled, the hardships, the refinement process, and often the isolation as everything swirled around me. The time in the fire fortified me to continue the journey and fueled the passion that was rising inside of me to overflowing. This same fire would burn away anything threatening to stifle the growth of new life. This fire of the Lord would be my everything, and many times I would feel like I had no more strength to continue.

You may have heard it said that God entrusts the most significant trials to his strongest soldiers, but the Bible states that God fights on our behalf; we are the tools he uses to defeat the enemy. And if we are indeed soldiers, then He is the captain of the army leading the charge. We are strong only because He is strong.

In Exodus 14:14, Moses tells the Israelites, "The LORD will fight for you; you need only to be still." This is in the context of the Israelites being trapped between the Red Sea and the Egyptian army. Moses is telling them to trust in God and not their abilities.

In our journey through life and its ups and downs, He is forging us, strengthening us, and sharpening us to wield us against the enemy; as He fights for us. This is what fuels my hope and my strength; especially on the dark, isolated days.

As you walk with me through my journey in this book, you will experience the full range of emotions from joy and sadness to hope and despair. It may be difficult for you at times because of the feelings that will come up and the flashbacks that may come up of your child. You may need to put the book down, take a walk, read scripture, pray, journal, get some sleep, cry, or do some vigorous exercise to work out those emotions. Embrace the flowing of feelings and emotions, recognize them, and honor them. Your outpouring of emotions is good—they are a testament to your connection to yourself and the love you shared with and for your child. Releasing emotions is an integral part of the grieving and healing journey. I will be here waiting for you to pick up the book again and continue the journey together.

Romans 5:3-5 is a good verse to meditate on during those times, "Not only that, but we rejoice in our sufferings, knowing that suffering produces endurance, and endurance produces character, and character produces hope, and hope does not put us to shame, because God's love has been poured into our hearts through the Holy Spirit who has been given to us."

My world completely changed the morning our family went from a family of 5 to a family of 4. The day had ended as usual the night before and the morning was starting out typical, as I got ready in the bathroom. But life can and does change in an instant.

It has been forever changed since, but one thing has remained the same — our faithful God. He has sustained, strengthened, sanctified, and reminded us daily of His sacrifice and resurrection. Guaranteeing our eternity in His presence, where he will wipe away every tear. Revelation 21:4

INTRODUCTION

Through this book, I want to point you to the One who will carry you from the base of your Mount Everest to the summit. Where you will hear, "Well done, good and faithful servant. You have been faithful over a little; I will set you over much. Enter into the joy of your master." Matthew 25:23

We can be confident that He is writing our story — my story, your story, and our child's story.

PART I: JOURNEY THROUGH THE WORST DAY

Going a little farther, he [Jesus] fell with his face to the ground and prayed, "My Father, if it is possible, may this cup be taken from me. Yet not as I will, but as you will."
Matthew 26:39

CHAPTER 1

THE BEST FAMILY WEEKEND

Grief has a way of making you irrationally focus on anything that you can control. That morning, as I was in the backyard scooping dog poop, my world had already shattered upstairs. My son's lifeless body lay under a sheet, and my mind was grasping for something—anything—to understand how it all led to this. To answer that question, I need to take you back to the days leading up to that unthinkable Tuesday morning on February 11, 2020.

The weekend before was busy for our family, but it was one that we had looked forward to. We were doing something together, all of us: Anthony, me, Alayna (15), Katelyn (12), and Jonathan (9). We had started to do things together more frequently, and it felt so good after many years of separation in our marriage. In addition, Anthony's dad, Dave, was in town for my eldest daughter, Alayna's, swim meet, which was scheduled for the next day.

We had initially planned to run the terrain race as a family, but unfortunately, Jonathan was not running with us because he had fractured his arm a few weeks before. Instead, he sat with his grandpa, playing games on his phone and cheering us on.

I think he was equally excited to do that, just sitting on a phone and playing games is not something he was allowed to do very often; as I tried to limit screen time as much as possible. We finished the race with mud all over us and had a great time laughing at our lack of coordination or ability to climb over a wall or crawl on our knees under a heavy rope.

It felt like we were entering into a new season as a family. Little did we know that this picture of us taken at the end of the race as a family of 4, minus Jonathan; would in just a few days, be our devastating and unexpected new normal.

After the race, we went to dinner at a pizza restaurant near our house, Anthony's Coal Fired Pizza. Unfortunately, owned by a different Anthony. Everyone was famished from all the energy we had expended during the race and was ready to have a good meal. As for Jonathan and Grandpa, I'm sure cheering us on was taxing as well.

We had a great time at the restaurant and left with full bellies. We were ready to relax at home before getting up early the next day for more physical activity. This time, the event would be an individual sport for Alayna; the rest of us would join J and Grandpa as spectators.

On Sunday morning, we all gathered at the competition pool to cheer Alayna on at her club swim meet. My mom, Maxine, joined us as well; she was visiting for the weekend from Ohio, where she lived with my older sister. There can be quite a few people at these events, sometimes with several clubs from all over Florida and tons of families there to cheer on each swimmer.

Alayna had been competing on her high school team and with a club team for a few years and had excelled at it, making it to Regional and State Competitions with her school. We were all very proud of her hard work, dedication, and commitment to push herself despite how tired she

CHAPTER 1

may be. Her coach also believed in her talent, but even more so in the quality of her character as a competitive athlete.

I remember Jonathan, whom we would affectionately call Buddy, or his other nickname, "J," was very fidgety that day and did not want to sit still in the stands. He kept complaining that he needed someone's phone to play on or wanted to go somewhere else and do something; as he had seen a playground nearby on our way to the pool earlier. It was often hard for him to wait patiently between his sister's races, as it could take a long time, and the race itself was relatively short because of the nature of the sport.

All parents of young kids can relate to weighing their decisions in a moment like that. Do I make him sit and practice self-control and discipline, or let him indulge his need to get energy out and create a fun time? We have so many moments like this in parenting at all stages; neither decision is right or wrong in the moment, but you may think your decision was/is right or wrong depending on what has happened since.

I wish I had taken the time to see him have fun and play on the playground instead of just sitting there waiting for the next race. As they say, "hindsight is 20/20". This is just one of the tiny moments I have had to release to the Lord; there are much bigger ones that I will share in the coming pages.

These are the last two photos that Katie, J's older sister and partner in crime, took of him breathing on that Sunday as he sat in the stands. There are a few that J also took of Katie, and I imagine looking straight through his eyes at his sister when I look at those. I noticed the night after his passing, as I looked back at the pictures, trying to get him to come back to me. I couldn't see his face in either photo. It was as if all I wanted was to see life in his eyes and a big, contagious smile on his face. Looking at these photos with his face not visible, makes me feel like I had already lost him at that point and just didn't know it yet.

After Alayna's race, Anthony took his dad to the airport to fly home to Indiana. My mom headed to West Palm Beach to visit friends. We had a wonderful weekend together, and it was a rare treat to have extended family on both sides around at the same time. Katie, Jonathan, and I waited for Alayna to do her cool-down exercises in the pool, get changed, and then we would go home to prepare for the week of school and work.

On the way home, we remembered that we hadn't been able to go to church earlier in the day; we decided to fit one more thing in and go to the night service after showering and getting dressed. Looking back, I don't recall anyone complaining or being too tired to go. It was a sweet time for us, enjoying church together, and it seemed like the cherry on top of the cupcake of a great weekend.

Originally Posted March 1, 2020 - 2 Days Before

I distinctly remember noticing how interested J was in everything going on around him. We were on the balcony, so he had a bird's eye view of the words to the songs in the back of the auditorium. The kids mentioned how they had never seen the back of the balcony so full. He watched as the grand piano was wheeled on and off stage, stayed entertained by the message, laughing at Pastor Dawn Chere Wilkerson and Rich learning to dance, and when the worship team got up, Jonathan leaned over to me and said, "The service is almost done, they just got up."

CHAPTER 1

I remember being so happy we had made it to the last service after a long, busy day and weekend. I remember smiling to myself at how much he was taking in, instead of me having to tell him to sit still.

> My little boy was growing up, and I was so proud.

As a Christian, you say the best is yet to come and know that it means once Jesus comes back, but you also think that means that this earthly life will continue to get better...

You forget that this is never promised to you. God does not promise you an easier, better earthly life once you invite him into your life. He just promises not to leave you or forsake you.

It's hard to find any better on this side of heaven when you wish everyone were already on the other side, especially when I was already more focused on eternal matters than temporary ones.

After church, we headed home to go to bed. During the busy weekend, Jonathan had wet his bed, which was the bottom bunk bed that he shared with his sister Katie. I hadn't taken the time to put the sheets back on his bed, so he was sleeping on an air mattress instead. Off to bed everyone went, and early the next morning we got up to head to school and work as usual.

    I hope that at this point you, my reader and now my friend on this journey, have been able to laugh and delight in the sweetness of these moments that we shared as a family. It is ok and good to be able to just sit in these moments and appreciate them for what they were, holding them tight and cherishing all the happiness and love without them being drowned out by the impending doom. As the verse below states, there is a season for rejoicing and celebration and a season of mourning; and each has its purpose. I welcome you to sit right here for a minute or two and cherish a special season you had with your family or child, whom you have lost. And it's ok, amidst the smiles and warm feelings, to allow a few tears of joy or sadness to accompany them too.

Scripture:
Ecclesiastes 3:1, "To everything, there is a season and a time for every purpose under heaven."

Prayer:
Lord, I thank you for my family, the time we get to spend together, and our love for each other. Laughing together, supporting each other, helping each other run our race well, and worshipping you together. Thank you for ultimately inviting us into your family and for being a Good Father. And as a good father, you promise to walk through every season with us. Amen

Reflection Questions:
1. What are some sweet memories that you can hold on to and thank the Lord for?
2. What do you need to release to the Lord/forgive yourself for from the days before?

CHAPTER 2

THE CALM BEFORE THE STORM

As I left J and K's room, I heard a still, small voice whisper in my ear, *"seizure"* ...and I ignored it. Instead, I walked downstairs to do the nightly routine as most mothers do after the kids go to bed. I'm sure you can quickly think of all the things on your list as well. Clean up the kitchen, get uniforms ready for the next morning, empty lunch boxes, and then mindlessly scroll on my phone when I know I should go to bed (what was I saying about screen time earlier? I should listen to my own advice, right?).

On this night, I was in the office watching videos of Bethel Church in California praying to raise Olive from the dead, a baby that had passed away. This story was making the national news as it had been many days since the baby passed away. Many across the country were watching in faith, and others with skepticism of what would happen or what God would do. I think I was more on the skeptics' side, but I was watching all the same.

It is ironic to me because when Jonathan's first seizures started back in May 2015, I was sitting on his bed massaging his leg because he was complaining that it was hurting. The kids had all just gone to bed after we had been at the beach all day. As I massaged his leg, I was reading about the Jonestown Massacre on my phone.

During his first and last seizures, stories of death were present in my mind and heart. I'm still not sure what to or not to read into this, but it's one of those anomalies. I wonder if it is an anomaly or something much deeper. In Ephesians 6:12, it says: "For we wrestle not against flesh and blood but against powers and principalities in this dark world". What was I wrestling in my house unaware? What had I welcomed in by fixating on these stories? I only recently started to think about these two occurrences in this way.

During his first seizure in 2015, I saw his eyes fly open, and he was just staring at the wall. I said to him, *"Jonathan, are you awake? Buddy??"* I picked him up, and his head stayed turned in that position like it was stuck; his body was limp, but his mouth was stiff as if his teeth were glued together and his jaw clenched. I ran into our master bedroom holding him in my arms, to wake Anthony. We then rushed everyone into the car and to the hospital.

As Anthony sped through the streets, we prayed that we wouldn't run any red lights, get stopped by police, or get into an accident. I sat in the back of the car with J in his car seat and placed my finger in his mouth to see if his jaw would relax.

I was constantly talking to him, praying, and trying to keep myself from hysterically bursting into tears uncontrollably. My mind was in disbelief at what had happened and what was happening to my son and our family.

By the time we got to the hospital, he was coming out of the seizure. He was drowsy but starting to talk, his jaw had relaxed, and his body was no longer limp. The staff tried to tell us that he was just sleepy. I insisted that it wasn't just that he was drowsy. They eventually agreed to admit us and then transferred us to another hospital, where we stayed for a few days.

Have you ever had to advocate for your child like that? I didn't understand how the doctors couldn't tell the difference between a child who just had a seizure and a child that's drowsy and sleepy. But I guess that's why some say to trust your mother's intuition above all else.

While we were there, I enlisted all the prayer warriors that I could and tried to keep Jonathan as entertained as possible. At this point he was back to his normal self and wanted to be out of the hospital and able to

CHAPTER 2

run around outside and play. They conducted an MRI test and an EEG, and everything came back normal; no tumor and no abnormal brain activity from what they could see. So, they discharged us, and we all prayed that we would never have to relive this ordeal again. The doctors said it could be a one-time thing, but they could not guarantee anything. We were grateful not to be facing a life-threatening diagnosis at that point, but we were now playing the wait-and-see game.

THE 2ND SEIZURE

But it did happen again...we finished the school year, and the kids went to visit their grandparents in Indiana for the summer. It was a tradition that they enjoyed because they were able to live a completely different life than they did living in the city of Miami. A welcome change of pace for them as they help their grandma on the farm with the animals, go out on the lake tubing with their grandpa, and run wild with their cousins. As all kids should be able to do, especially during the summer.

It was also an opportunity for Anthony and me to have time alone, which was rare during the school year. We had quickly welcomed our eldest, Alayna, after getting married, so we never had a lot of time just being newlyweds. Summer and sometimes Christmas break were glimpses of what our life together before kids maybe would have looked like.

We all enjoyed summer break and suddenly it was over in the blink of an eye, and they arrived back home at the Miami airport. Anthony and I picked them up and were driving home; Buddy was holding my hand because he missed me, then the 2nd seizure happened. We were talking to him, and I turned around and noticed that his eyes were off to one side and his jaw was clenched. Our hearts stopped; we had all been enjoying being reunited, but the moment quickly spiraled into tragedy.

We pulled over and called an ambulance, which never showed up. Our friend Jaime told us to drive him to the hospital where she was working. By the time we got there, he was coming out of the seizure, like how it happened the first time.

They admitted him, and we went through a range of tests again. Ultimately, they couldn't tell us what was causing them. The doctors said they are often caused by exhaustion, dehydration, or overstimulation. And because this is now his 2nd in a matter of a few months; they recommended that he go on preventative medication. Our life was changed forever. Truthfully, it had changed at the first seizure, as the pending doom of a second one was always hanging over our heads. Now, with the prescribing of preventative medication, there was a good chance that it would happen again. So, our journey with seizures officially began.

Coming back to the present, here we were on the Monday night before the fateful morning. The morning, we didn't know was coming but it was always our biggest fear. When I walked upstairs to go to bed, it was at least 1am. Instead of checking on Jonathan, like the still, small voice had warned me to; I walked right past his room door and into mine. Maybe he was sleeping peacefully, and maybe he was already in the arms of Jesus. I will never know.

Originally Posted March 5, 2020 -The Calm Before The Storm

In the what-ifs, guilt, and regret from that day, there are little things that make me feel closer to Jonathan. I remember the specifics of that last day with him in such detail.

This picture was taken on one of our many trips to Aldi together. The kids have a love/hate relationship with Aldi because they miss the name brands but are so happy when I come home with double what we could afford to buy elsewhere.

CHAPTER 2

So that Monday evening, February 10th, I picked up J and K from school and got Chicken Kitchen for dinner. We had scraped together lunches that morning, but we got extra CK for lunch the next day because I hadn't gone to Aldi yet after the busy weekend.

I knew that Jonathan was not thrilled to take CK, so I told him I would go to Aldi while Katie was at piano lessons. He and Alayna would stay home to eat, bathe, and do homework. After coming home from Aldi and piano lessons with Katie, I helped him finish up some math. There were a few problems we were going to finish in the morning.

I remember telling him how smart he was, I didn't have to explain each one to him. We cut his fingernails before bed, and I told him that I was going to bathe him the next day because obviously it was hard for him with one hand, since he had a cast on the other.

After tucking him in, he would often realize he hadn't fed his fish, "Wait, Mom, can you feed my fish? Just three pebbles". Most nights, I told him he could feed him in the morning. That night, I told him ok. He said, "What about devotions?" and because it was late, I told him we would do it tomorrow.

> I told him one last time that I loved him and J, K and I said our nightly routine, "I love you, God loves you more, sweet dreams, sleep tight, don't let the bed bugs bite and I'll see you in the morning."

It may be silly, and I know when he woke up in Jesus' arms, it didn't matter to him anymore. But it brings me some peace that he fell asleep knowing his fish was fed, that he didn't have to have Chicken Kitchen for lunch the next day and that he was so loved.

Friend, I know that as I recall these events, I can feel the buildup in my heart and chest, and I imagine that this may be happening to you as well. You also may be reflecting on the road that you are walking on. Take time to step away if you need to; my desire is not to spread fear or anxiety in your heart but to connect with you through my story. I like to reflect on this verse from Isaiah at times like this. I know whatever I am about to walk through or into, I do not need to fear, for the Lord is with me and will uphold me. Tissue comes in handy as well, so if you don't have any, then you may want to grab some as we proceed into some harder parts of my journey.

Scripture:
Isaiah 41:10, "Fear not, for I am with you; be not dismayed, for I am your God; I will strengthen you, I will help you, I will uphold you with my righteous right hand."

Prayer:
Lord, thank you for speaking to me in a still, small voice; thank you for continuing to speak to me even to this day. I may not understand all that transpired that night; there are so many things that I would go back and change, and I know that my responsibility is to trust you and lean on you when I fall into the what ifs. You are sovereign over all, and you are working all for my good and your glory. Amen

Reflection Questions:
1. Can you recall any still, small voice moments in the days leading up to the day?
2. Is there something(s) that you are thankful for during that time?

CHAPTER 3

THE SADDEST DARKEST DAY

Tuesday, February 11th started the same as many other mornings that school year. We often take the uneventful, mundane, routine moments for granted, often forgetting how they can instantly change everything about the future.

I was in the bathroom getting ready; Alayna went to wake her siblings up as she always had done as their big sister. As she proceeded into J and K's room, she screamed for me to come because something was very wrong; Buddy wasn't waking up. Anthony was downstairs making lunches and breakfast. I screamed his name as I entered their room, where Katie and Alayna stood shocked as they had just experienced the end that we had been so close to several times before.

I can't imagine what they had to deal with at that moment as children. Even as an adult, I know it was an unbearable situation for my mind to wrap around. All the times before this, we were given the gift of getting to hug him after a seizure and tell him how he had scared us.

Most times, he would be completely unaware of the occurrence. Other times, he may have a headache or feel very fatigued after, but this time was different. There would be no conversation with him afterward, if the reality of what we were seeing was too far gone and irreversible. I texted my mom and sister, *"Please pray"*. No details and no explanation; I had no other words in that moment, just pray. It was all I could convey, maybe I knew that everything else was pointless, and explaining more would make it too real.

Did you experience this as well? Were you speechless in the moment? I understand that a lot of people experience this as their mind is trying to catch up with what has and is quickly unfolding in front of them. Everything happens faster than our mind and heart can comprehend.

As Anthony ran upstairs to answer my screams and entered J and K's room, he immediately shouted to call 911. Buddy was unresponsive, and we both cried profusely as we pleaded with him to hold on and please don't go. As the dispatcher answered, we sobbed as we described the scene we had walked into and was continuing to unfold in front of us.

The female voice on the other side of the phone walked Anthony through administering cpr in case we were able to bring him back before help got to us. She asked us to describe what we were seeing as Anthony pressed on his chest and blew into his mouth. He told her that foam was coming from his mouth. We didn't know if that was a good sign or not, but we continued to follow her instructions, as we were otherwise helpless at this moment.

During this time, I started to hear sirens in the distance. As they got closer, I ran downstairs to flag them down but they couldn't get through the gate. *"Where was the gate opener? Just call somebody on the keypad, every second is important!"*, was running through my brain.

When they finally got in, they ran upstairs, and we told the girls to wait downstairs. We were trying to protect them from at least seeing the police officers work on their brother's body; we were trying to protect them from further trauma. However, none of us were protected in this situation; we would be forever affected by this in big and small ways. I texted my neighbor Beatriz, asking if the girls could come to her house, but there was no reply. It just so happened that her phone was dead at the time. I can't imagine what the girls were feeling sitting down there alone by themselves after witnessing what they had.

I think looking back, their well-being was forgotten during this time as we tried to save their brother's life. It's kind of how they tell you to treat the most critical patients first. But that doesn't mean that minor issues are not compounding in less critical patients at that moment as well.

CHAPTER 3

The effects of this moment would compound in each of us for the rest of our lives. Would it be a crippling loss that would debilitate us, or would it be a loss that propelled us into our passion and purpose? This was yet to be seen.

The police officers finally ran upstairs and tried to detect a pulse and took over doing cpr on Jonathan. They ushered us out of the room into the hallway. We cried as we watched them for a few minutes. The situation was not getting any better, and the reality of J being gone started to set in. That's when the paramedics arrived, and there was a brief moment of an inkling of hope. He greeted us, turned to go into J and K's room, and immediately turned back around. His face fell, and he said, *"I am so sorry; he is already gone."*

Those were the most heartbreaking, soul-crushing words we had ever heard; every ounce of hope was gone forever. Anthony immediately punched the bathroom door and shouted, *"My son is dead!"* We both cried uncontrollably, and I'm sure we were both repeating in our heads, *"No, No, No, No, No!"*.

I proceeded to gain my composure enough to ask the paramedic how long he thought he had been gone. I was trying to formulate a timeline in my head, trying to get some information about the situation that we had suddenly been thrust into. All the while in the back of my head, thinking about that small voice that I had ignored the night before. The paramedic, however, had no specific answers for me. He said, *"Maybe a few hours because you can see his blood pooling in his legs as it is not being pumped through his body any longer, and the pooling takes a few hours."* He was very caring in his demeanor, he tried to calm us and console us as much as possible, and answer any questions that we may have about a funeral home, etc. But all we wanted to do was turn back time, start this day over, and wake up from the most horrible nightmare. But there was no way to do any of those things; we were completely helpless in this situation.

The police officer and paramedic gave their condolences and proceeded to cover his body with a sheet. Anthony and I went back into his room to cry and say how sorry we were for not being there for him and ask over and over how this was real. At that moment, I looked at Anthony and said, *"The girls are downstairs by themselves"*. He immediately got up from the floor next to Buddy's body and went down to sit and cry with them. He confirmed the new reality they feared was unfolding but would give anything to undo.

BUDDY IS GONE

I stayed with Buddy and texted my sister and mom, *"Buddy is gone."* Again, I found it hard to share much more with those who were not in person and were experiencing this with us. But I felt they deserved some sort of update to know how to pray now; we were no longer praying for the resuscitation of Jonathan's body; we were now praying that this wouldn't take us all out with him.

A few minutes later, my neighbor Beatriz left her house across the street to take her girls to school, unaware of what had transpired, not even 100 feet away. As she came around the small roundabout, she saw the police cars in our driveway. As soon as she passed our driveway, her phone came alive as it began to charge. The moment she read my message on her phone lock screen, she stopped the car right away and ran up to our door, leaving her girls in the car. I honestly don't remember how I ended up downstairs in the driveway to tell her about the news with the girls, but we all fell into each other's arms and cried profusely together in disbelief. She immediately had her husband, Doug, take her girls to school, and she scooped my girls up and took them to her house for refuge.

I headed back upstairs to finish with the police and do the only thing that I could do for Jonathan — sit with his body. I knew he wasn't there any longer, but I felt that I had abandoned him in his last moments. So, I would do my best to take care of the last thing I had of him and ensure that I fulfilled my responsibilities.

While sitting there, I was rehearsing everything in my head and feeling like I had failed immensely at all my responsibilities thus far, and the worst had come to pass. How could I ever trust myself again? Have you experienced a moment of feeling completely untrustworthy? I have struggled with this my entire life, and it had come to a head in my deepest failure.

CHAPTER 3

Up until this moment, the only communication outside of our bubble of us and the neighbors had been minimal, and it was time to fill in all the details for the closest people to us. Each conversation brought it more into reality; the wider the news went, the more collateral damage there was. The more hearts that were breaking; the more worlds had been changed forever. I stayed with Jonathan's body, holding his shoulder, crying and apologizing repeatedly. Until my mother arrived at the house. and promptly told me that it wasn't good for me to sit there with his body.

I told her he had been all alone when he passed, but I think she misunderstood what I said through my sobs and thought I said that he was all alone in that room at that moment. I don't know if it was right for me to stay with his body or to leave it; I don't know if there are any right or wrongs in those moments or the moments that would follow. But that would be the last time that I, as his mother, spent time alone with Jonathan in any way. He was now all alone on the 2nd floor of our house, and we were all downstairs.

What are we to do now? How does life just continue? We were walking into uncharted waters, or rather, being pushed into the onslaught of what felt like a tsunami of unknowns that could overtake us.

Within the next few hours, our closest friends were notified, and they began to drop what they were doing and ran to our side. Each one loved Buddy as a son, a nephew, and a brother to their children and suffered this loss as if it were their child who had passed away.

As helpless as I felt in the situation, that's when I decided that something I could accomplish was cleaning up the poop in the backyard. It was an ongoing problem of the kids letting Charlie out into the backyard instead of walking him on the street, and as much as we would tell them to pick up the poop after him...it never happened.

So now here it was that people would be coming to my house, and there would be poop everywhere. I knew then and still know now that focusing on this at that moment was irrational, but everything else in that situation was completely out of my control. I needed to feel like I could control something.

I was the one who usually posts on social media, but today, Anthony announced it to a wider audience of family and friends far away. All I could do was share his post. I had no words to add at that moment, but the words would start to flow soon afterward and ultimately would make up a large portion of this book. Everyone near and far shared our shock and immediate heartbreak. In those pictures, you could see the love we shared, the huge smile that displayed the excitement for life that Jonathan had, the hopes and dreams that he had for his life, and the hopes we had for him and us all together. That hope had been shattered in a moment.

As the news spread, the outpouring of love and support was just as immediate. From old and new friends, work colleagues, bosses, churches, both of our extended families, friends of friends, teachers and coaches, and even strangers were sending their condolences. Their support wasn't just in words, but it came in every way that you could imagine, each person giving what they could in that moment. From monetary donations, food, time spent, and favors called in from all over to ensure that we had everything we needed. Everyone knew that there was only one thing we needed or even wanted in that moment, our Jonathan back with us, and simultaneously, we all knew none of them could provide that.

HERE COME THE HELPERS

My friend Natalie was the first one to arrive at my house, I have known her for all 20 years of living in Miami. We worked together prior and had babies at the same time. We parented each other's kids during the hardest years of having little ones; and she affectionately calls my mother— Granmax.

CHAPTER 3

Jamie and Kristina were next. Jamie is one of the kindest, most welcoming people you will ever meet. She takes in all the orphans, and we often felt like that in Miami. She always had a house full of kids and the parents were just as welcome, too. Jamie helped to locate and call the funeral home; communicating and organizing the most heart-wrenching request we ever had to navigate. I couldn't have done it without her help.

When Kristina arrived, I told her that this was the one thing that I had never wanted to have in common with her. She too, had lost her son; his name was Gavin, and he was an infant when he passed away. Similar loss but a different situation. No matter the situation, burying your child as a parent is a club that you never want to be a part of. Our girls had met in Pre-K, and even though their friendship had a rocky start, they had been joined at the hip and heart for the past 7 years.

My friendships with them and our girls' friendships have continued to blossom and grow as life has provided many valleys and mountain-top moments since this day. Which is one of the few constants we can count on in this life.

During our wait for the funeral home attendants to arrive, we all prayed in a circle in the backyard with my girls, my mom, and Anthony. We thanked the Lord for who He was; we thanked Him for never leaving us or forsaking us and for providing a way for us to be reunited with Him and each other. We asked him for comfort, peace, and joy so that His gospel could be proclaimed and for Him to be glorified. We thanked Him for using everything for our good.

Throughout this situation, I never blamed God for taking my son; I never thought I was being punished or that God was being mean. I fully understood that we live in a fallen world, and this was a consequence of sin and death. Thanks to the Lord for His plan of redemption and salvation. This was never God's original plan, but I am thankful for his redemptive plan.

I know that this is not always the reaction to God in these moments, and there were times that I had to remind myself of the truths that we prayed and declared that morning. However, this truth was my anchor during this time and even to this day. It would be the hope that I hold on to, my life raft, the wind beneath my wings, the engine to propel me home.

Those all sound like clichés, but I have experienced them all at different times. I have felt the truth of God's word, His character, and His love sustaining me and guiding me every day, just as he had all the days before this fateful Tuesday morning in 2020.

The time in between Jamie calling the funeral home and them arriving to take J's body was like an out-of-body experience; as if I was watching it all unfold, and it wasn't happening to me. We sat downstairs and talked about her 12-year-old daughter Ava, who at the time had a "boyfriend" who was in another state. She set up a GoFundMe for our family, and I really can't remember what else she, Natalie, Kristina, and I talked about. What do you even talk about in those moments?

I remember seeing Anthony pacing in the backyard, getting calls on and off, and them saying to me that I needed to take care of him and make sure he was okay because he was taking it hard. We all needed to look out for each other as we navigated this road together, and inevitably, we would have to walk our own roads as well. We would have to wrestle with our own feelings and emotions, questions and doubts within ourselves, and find our way to let them out.

While we waited, my pastor's wife from church called; it was such a sweet surprise, as we didn't go to a small church. I had spoken to her during other times about my marriage struggles, but I wasn't sure if she knew who I was or our family. All 3 of my kids were well known in the kids' ministry, though. And several different church members who were friends and in servant leadership roles reached out and offered prayers and support. We experienced how a very large church can still feel small and intimate when the Lord has joined your hearts together, in good times and bad.

TIME TO TAKE THE BODY

The dreaded moment was here; they knocked on the door, and it was time. We called the girls and our neighbor, Beatriz, to come over from the neighbor's house across the street to say our goodbyes. We all waited downstairs while they went upstairs to carry him down. I was physically

CHAPTER 3

and visibly shaking as we waited and had to use the wall to hold myself up, so I didn't collapse to the floor.

The initial tension and adrenaline in my body from earlier that morning, when discovering Jonathan lifeless on the air mattress, had subsided as we were waiting for the next step in this unimaginable situation. All that adrenaline came rushing back in an instant. Perhaps my body thought that if this step of them taking his body never came, we could somehow go back to normal. Reality rushed back in as they headed upstairs to do a job that I don't know how anyone would willingly choose.

They used the sheet that had been on the air mattress that Buddy was sleeping on the night before, to wrap his body. He was completely stiff as two people carried him slowly down the steep stairs to put him on the gurney. As a family of 4, we said goodbye to our littlest family member, and of course, another round of weeping ensued. I remember asking about an autopsy and was told that it wasn't customary unless foul play was suspected. I also asked about organ donation, but that must happen while the organs are still functioning.

In my mind, I was still trying to organize and rationalize the situation and redeem it in our world. Maybe I could bring some understanding or "good" out of a seemingly only horrible situation. I would quickly realize that that was not my job and a weight that I could never bear.

That was the last time that Jonathan's body was ever in our home; the last time that the girls and I saw him. He was now gone forever, never to return.

Hey friend, I'm checking in on you as you walk through my telling of this journey. I have had time to reflect on all parts of my story over and over. I have learned over the years of sharing my story, my audience can feel the shock of that morning all at once, and I need to be sensitive to that. Kind of like the first time you watch a movie and the impact the events and story can have on you.

At this point, I have the gift of looking back and knowing how far I have come, as the verse in Romans 8 says, "In all things, we are more than conquerors through him who loved us. For I am sure that neither death nor life...will be able to separate us from the love of God in Christ Jesus our Lord."

I am a conqueror, and so are you. Wherever you find yourself on your journey, hold on to this promise. It will anchor you in your most challenging moments and pull you out of your deepest despair.

Scripture:
Romans 8:37-39, "No, in all these things, we are more than conquerors through him who loved us. For I am sure that neither death nor life, nor angels nor rulers, nor things present nor things to come, nor powers, nor height nor depth, nor anything else in all creation, will be able to separate us from the love of God in Christ Jesus our Lord."

Prayer:
Lord, I thank you that we are never separated from your love, no matter the circumstances. Your love casts out all fear, sustains us, and reminds us that you have made a way, and your blood redeems creation. I also thank you for welcoming us to express all that we are to you; we do not need to hide our emotions, questions, or doubts from you. Amen

CHAPTER 3

Reflection Questions:
1. Can you remember the details of that day, or is it all a blur?
2. Despite everything that you likely want to forget from that day, is there anything that you want to hold on to?
3. What were you feeling or were you numb?
4. Who supported you most?
5. Were you or are you angry at God? Have you spoken to Him about it?

CHAPTER 4

THE GATHERING OF OUR BROKEN HEARTS

I don't recall when more people started gathering at our house that day, but I know there was a steady stream of friends and family of all ages going in and out. Many friends brought or sent food and flowers; and many calls and texts were received. It was a strange thing, as I am more reserved and private, to now be mourning in very physical, emotional, and spiritual ways in public with others.

We also had to be entertaining and fellowshipping with people who came to comfort and uplift us and remind us that we were not alone. It's a fine line between wanting to be all alone to cry and grieve and knowing that this is a collective grief as well.

One way to overcome that grief is to cherish the love you share with those you are still walking this life with. When they hug you, many times it's because they need that hug too. It was a beautiful moment to support each other in our weakness, as our hearts broke together repeatedly.

I remember my other friend, Christina with a "C", telling me that if I just wanted to be by myself, that was fine too. She could see that my mind and heart kept wandering while standing in a room full of people.

I replied, *"No, it's okay. I just think I'm a little out of small talk and emotionally and physically exhausted, as this started very early this morning."*

SETTLING IN FOR THE NIGHT

As everyone left for the night and the friends and family that came to be with us from out of town settled in, we tried to go to bed ourselves. I don't remember where Katie slept that night; I can't imagine she slept in her room. I will have to ask her. I remember as I laid down and closed my eyes, I would see Buddy's body. My chest would get so tight, I would sob uncontrollably, and I could barely breathe. Anthony just held me as we cried together; it was all we could do, and there was no stopping the tears, even if we tried.

I'm not sure when I fell asleep that night, but before I did, I posted the pictures in my stories from chapter 1 of Jonathan. The ones from two days before at Alayna's swim meet.

I wished with all that I was that he would come back to me, that I would see his sweet smile again, but even in these pictures, his smile was hidden from me. I cried to sleep, hoping that when I woke, I would be waking from what was surely only a nightmare.

Daybreak came and I woke up violently from my sleep and immediately burst into tears; I could barely breathe as reality flooded back into my conscious mind. I felt like I was hyperventilating and couldn't stop shaking. Each time the shock hit me; it was worse than before.

OUR STREET

Anthony took me outside to walk, to release some of that energy out of my body; my legs could barely hold me up. He had to hold me to keep me from falling to the ground as we walked in circles around our one street.

As we walked, I commented on how Jonathan was all alone when he died. Anthony told me that if there was anyone who believed that wasn't

CHAPTER 4

true, he knew it was me. He knew I thought Jesus and my dad were waiting for Jonathan, to welcome him home into heaven.

Ultimately, that was what I believed, but I felt guilty for him being alone on this side of eternity; I felt like I had failed him. The street we walked on was where Jonathan had learned to ride a bike without training wheels. The street that he and his sisters would play for hours with the neighbors, who had become family. The street that has been instrumental in who my kids are, is both a reminder of countless happy times and now one moment in time that would forever change them. Would this one life-changing, tragic moment now overshadow all the happy moments from before? Would there be any pleasant times on this street again? Or would there always be a cloud hanging over our street?

None of us knew it yet, but this street was about to become a bubble for our family from the pressure of society as we grieved and the imminent threat of Covid-19, which was about to change everyone's life. What everyone else would think of as a restriction, I would view as a gift to my family of incubation to heal and emerge slowly back into society and everyday life—more on that later.

We moved to this street in March 2017. Anthony and I had battled through another rough season of our marriage and were going to marriage counseling. We were paying off debt and were able to move our family out of the tiny two-bedroom townhouse that we had been living in and where Jonathan had his first seizure 2 years before.

We saw a house on this street listed for rent online. So, after we had gone to the movies on a date, we snuck in the gate. There was a lovely elderly neighbor lady, Sonia, outside in her yard when we were driving by. We stopped and asked her if she knew the people renting it and any details. Within minutes she told us that she had the key and asked if we wanted to see inside. We looked at each other and knew that it was a divine appointment. We felt an attachment right away, and it all worked out very quickly.

It was a fresh start for our family. We could have a little more room to spread out and organize our things, so they weren't all over the place all the time. It had a pool in the backyard, so we could have hours of endless entertainment, and it was much closer to the kids' school.

Within a few days of us moving in, we heard a knock on the door. It was the family from across the street, the Alvarengas, welcoming us to the neighborhood with freshly baked chocolate chip cookies. They quickly became known as "The Neighbors" and a staple in our everyday lives. Impromptu dinners and sleepovers, movie sessions and dance parties, ice cream runs, bundt cake birthdays, and eating a whole watermelon in the driveway were among the common shared activities. Buddy was always watching for when they would come home to see if they could play; he had gained 2 more sisters and was so happy to have them. The kids often joked about stringing a "telephone" made of string and cups across the street from house to house so they could always communicate. I'm sure they would have thought digging underground tunnels would be a great idea, too.

Back in the present—the next few days were kind of a cycle through times of crying and numbness, trying to organize the celebration of life for Buddy, communicate with friends and family, and spend time with the friends and family who were in town.

Playing worship music while just sitting at the dining table and letting the songs minister to my heart, became a time of great healing early on. I will share some of those songs with you and pray that they will do the same for you. It was a strange feeling of being so grateful to spend that time with everyone, because there were people in my house who had never been there before. Such as Anthony's friend Phil from Indiana had never even flown on a plane before. But as soon as he heard the news of Jonathan's passing, he knew he needed to be there to comfort his childhood best friend.

Anthony's dad had just gotten home to Indiana, from being in town over the weekend, as I talked about earlier in my story. He and his wife came right back as soon as they received the news. Dave kept saying how grateful he was to have had that time with Jonathan just a few days before, a true gift to him from the Lord. Everyone could see that amidst such great pain; there were also blessings mingled throughout.

CHAPTER 4

FAMILY + PLANNING

My sister, Rachel, and her family had been helping to comfort and organize from afar and arrived in town from Ohio a few days after the fateful Tuesday morning. She walked in holding baby Avery, who never got to know Jonathan on a real level but talks about him all the time now as if she did. Avery also has a special love for our dog Charlie, and I think she somehow knows that Charlie and Jonathan shared a special love and were best buds. Zoe walked in ready to keep J's memory alive for all to remember him exactly how she knew and loved him, as Naked boy. He was always only wearing his underwear as soon as he walked through the door of our house and always joking around.

My sister walked in, and as the 2nd mother to all my children as soon as they were born, she immediately felt the weight of what she had been holding from afar coming crashing down upon her, as reality set in. As Adam, my brother-in-law, walked in, I realized that he and I had just started to see J flourish in different ways. He had started to take him on his plane and show him more boy stuff as he was getting older. We had discussed exploring different treatments that Anthony and I had investigated, and suddenly, all that was gone. There was no longer any need for those treatments but also gone was the hope that the treatments could possibly have provided.

We were so blessed to have my good friends Jesus and Blanca, who went to the funeral home to help make arrangements for J's body and happened to be there when my mom and Beatriz stopped by. So many were trying to help us find a sanctuary to host the celebration; our church at the time did not have a building of its own. The hunt was on; and we were surprised that places were either booked, too small, too large, or too far.

Decisions like the design for our Team Simpson shirts, planning the agenda, picking photos to print that show his personality, designing the flyer, partnering with friends to organize food, bookmarks, location for the service, who will speak and what worship songs we will proclaim into our reality—we're all things that we were discussing during this time. These things seemed like all we could control in an uncontrollable situation; they gave us some sense of purpose and direction to keep us moving amidst the fear of falling into despair.

The visit Anthony, my mom, and I took to the funeral home was extremely difficult. Picking out the casket to bury J in, as if in the end it really mattered. But as soon as we saw the black one, we knew it was "perfect"; it looked like it was straight out of Black Panther. It's strange to say that about a casket, but it warmed our hearts that even in this decision, we could put love and care into it.

We knew the black one was perfect because it seemed like what a superhero would be buried in; Jonathan loved the Avengers and so many others. We found some big Avengers stickers online to put on it, to complete the look. We gave J a proper Avengers burial, as every superhero should get.

Next was the burial plot. The scene of us driving around choosing a plot in the cemetery was surreal, as we thought that a more serene area would help to mend our broken hearts when we visited. During the meeting, Anthony also wrestled with the idea that because this horrible thing had happened, surely something else was on the way. He asked, *"Should we buy the double plot to prepare for the next tragedy?"* My mom, who had accompanied us, and I quickly had to remind him that you can't live life like that, always looking for tragedy and heartbreak around every corner.

But if I'm honest, I had lived a lot of my life like that before this, so I was preaching to myself. And somehow, now that the seemingly worst tragedy had happened, I was being freed of that fear. I was realizing that I couldn't control anything, no matter how much I tried, and worrying about it wouldn't help either. Life has these unexpected gifts and lessons it brings us at the most unexpected times.

We decided on a plot near a pond with turtles and fish. Anthony joked about painting a shield on a turtle shell in tribute to Buddy, our superhero. This area had more trees than others, and wind chimes in a tree nearby; it sounded like the angels were singing when the wind blew. I think it gave the illusion of life flourishing, where other areas felt like a desert because of the lack of foliage.

We chose an area based on what our hearts needed and wanted at that time, and not an area that would reflect the desert of how we truly

CHAPTER 4

were feeling inside. In the midst of how difficult those meetings were physically and emotionally; we were so blessed to have 2 angels working with us; they truly showed God's love and peace. I made a point to ask questions about their personal/work life and thanked them so much for their care and kindness. I told them, *"I wish that I had never met them in these circumstances, but it was a pleasure meeting them"*. During this journey, especially early on, it was our village or community that helped us navigate the road ahead and carry the great weight that had been placed on our shoulders.

Maybe you experienced the same, or maybe you didn't. How can you be the person you needed during that time? Or whose example in your life can you follow? Whether we go through a similar tragedy or can't relate at all, it is hard for us all to know what to do or say in those moments. It is a time for us to give ourselves and others grace. It is also a great opportunity to see people walking in their gifts that the Lord has given them. Some which include hospitality, organization, compassion, empathy, counseling, cooking, cleaning, and even just listening. I know I had a host of prayer warriors behind the scenes holding me up as well.

How are you doing at this point, friend? We have walked through some very difficult experiences together, and the next is difficult as well as we lay Jonathan in his final resting place. Do you need to take a break or a walk? It's ok if you do, to ensure that you are processing what you are feeling along the way.

Scripture:
Galatians 6:2, "Bear one another's burdens, and so fulfill the law of Christ."

Prayer:
Lord, I thank you for your body of Christ and even those who don't know you; thank you for placing your characteristics of caring for one another in our hearts. For it is in our weakness, you make us strong, and many times that is through people in our lives who step in to help. May we be people who are eager to help others as well, to give of ourselves, to shine our light and love. And when we feel we don't have anyone and at times truly don't, may we know that you are always with us. You will never leave us or forsake us. Amen

Reflection Questions:
1. Do you tend to be more private or public with your feelings?
2. Did you struggle the first night going to sleep or the first morning waking up?
3. What did you do to get the energy or tension out of your body?
4. What were some things said to you during the fellowship in the following days?
5. What special moments or things did you have at the Funeral or Celebration of their life?

CHAPTER 5

THE CELEBRATION + BURIAL

With the logistics of Jonathan's final resting place decided and arranged, it was time for the next phase of planning for the Celebration of Life. Amidst the scurry of entertaining friends and family, pulling myself out of the deep depths of despair to leave my bed, and enjoying those visiting from near and far. Leaning on the truths of God's word and reminding myself that Jonathan was now with his savior, free of seizures, free of sadness, free of everything broken in this world—was anchoring me during this time. All the planning kept me distracted, and it almost felt like walking through a dream. Like we weren't really preparing a night to somehow seek and invite others into closure, but we were just giving Jonathan the birthday party he had always deserved.

J's birthday was always around Thanksgiving, and with my job being retail, family time during the holidays is pretty much non-existent. Plus, everyone else is traveling and busy too.

The year prior (2019), we had managed to have a small last-minute party for him, and I am so glad that his friends have that memory of that special time with him. We went to Skyzone, where you can jump and play games on trampolines, a favorite place of his. He was always jumping and bouncing all over the place instead of standing still in everyday life, and at Skyzone, you can jump extra high and run around as much as you want.

I imagine he's bouncing from cloud to cloud in heaven and testing his turbo speed, if he has those options. After Skyzone, we went to a nearby park for pizza and cupcakes. You could see that he felt so special and very excited to be celebrated with more than just a cake and our family on Thanksgiving Day.

"Happy last birthday on this earth, Buddy, we love you."

xoxo,
Mom, Dad, Alayna, and Katie

CELEBRATION OF LIFE

For the ceremony, Anthony and I wanted to have oversized pictures that showed Buddy's personality and different stages of life, so we headed to FedEx Print and Ship to order them. We were very indecisive and took a long-time choosing materials and sizes with the employee at the counter. Behind us stood one young man very patiently for a good 30 minutes, not saying anything or showing any sign of frustration. Once we were done and left the store, the young man followed us and said, *"Ex-*

CHAPTER 5

cuse me, are you Jonathan Simpson's parents?" Anthony and I looked at each other in surprise and said, *"Yes, we are, and you look familiar"*.

He then shared with us that he was an after-school care teacher last year, and Jonathan was one of his students. He went on to tell us how Jonathan was so fun and an awesome kid, whom he will never forget. He told us how one time another kid was creating some mischief, and he jokingly blamed it on Jonathan, making him laugh. He loved Jonathan's expressions and laughter.

Our grief momentarily turned to laughter, followed by a gratefulness that this young man took the time to come out of the store and tell us about his experiences with Jonathan and the impression he had left on him. We got in our car and looked at each other with happy tears in our eyes. It felt good running into a seemingly random person 25 minutes from his school. Whom the Lord used to bring comfort, joy, and laughter. I know that it was not random at all, though; the Lord was taking care of us in so many ways throughout this journey.

Now, back to planning. The first thing I knew was that I didn't want his celebration to be stuffy and depressing; it needed to be kid-friendly, as there would be kids of all ages attending. It would be a tribute to Buddy with bright colored balloons and everyone wearing superhero shirts. I would design the flyer, and we would send it out to everyone, the more the merrier.

We even went to their old elementary school, Leewood K-8, to visit the teachers, principal, and office staff. We wanted to invite them and sit with them for a moment, as they had collected cards for our family. Leewood was like one big family when the kids attended there, and I knew that they would make sure that everyone who wanted to attend, knew all the details.

Kristina would coordinate the food, which her boss contributed. She also designed a bookmark for people to take home with them to have a keepsake of Buddy. We decided to put John 3:16 on them, as our greatest desire was to share and highlight the Gospel in every way that we could. I still have people tell me that they have it displayed on their fridge and that they pray for our family whenever they look at it. Extras were handed out on Easter, placed in book bags during a school supply drive, and I have one in multiple books and in my Bible. It's nice to open my Bible and have a reminder of Buddy and the Gospel to anchor me.

My sister even laminated one for each of her girls so they wouldn't get ruined and so they could keep them for many years to come. Speaking of years, it's hard to believe it has been 5 years already at the time of me writing this in 2025. At the same time, so much has changed since that fateful Tuesday morning in February 2020.

My other friend, Christina, helped me plan the details of the ceremony, once we finally found the location. We tried to find somewhere closer, but we ended up in the church building of the dad of our pastors. We felt at home, cared for and right where we were supposed to be. Other friends offered to make superhero t-shirts for our now family of 4, on the back it read —Team Simpson - Underneath are the Everlasting arms. Deuteronomy 33:27.

The day before we had the large gathering together with friends from near and far, Alayna's JCC swim team hosted a special balloon release ceremony. It was the first time, outside of our house, that we were gathering with a group of people. We all felt a little uncomfortable, the feeling of constant gratitude for everyone showing up for you but wishing that it wasn't for this reason.

They also made us silicone bracelets that said, *"Gone, But Never Forgotten."* We wore them for a very long time after; the girls would ask me for a new one when their's would break. Like somehow it was keeping his memory alive and us connected to him. It was also a little reminder of all the people in that area of Alayna's life, that Buddy and our family had touched.

Then the night we had been planning for a week had arrived, and everything was a fog to me. I barely cried because I didn't have any more tears to cry; and was just emotionally and physically exhausted as well. There were all these people, whom we love, around us hurting too and wanting to comfort us but were needing comfort themselves. And in some ways, they were just now fully facing what we had navigated for 9 days at this point. They had the "gift" of distance from reality until now.

Our girls, especially, were navigating the most difficult road. Anthony and I sat them down and told them it was ok for this night to be whatever they needed it to be. That they did not need to be afraid to cry

CHAPTER 5

because of fear that people would be watching. We were all there to mourn and support each other and celebrate our love for Jonathan. Even Anthony's mom, who had never flown before, took her first flight to come and be with our family. Miracles and healing were happening in all different ways, and some we won't see or know about until eternity.

I knew that this night was much bigger than just about Jonathan. I knew that God had a chance to plant and cultivate seeds that had been planted in people's hearts. I prayed that He would be glorified and that peace, joy, and fulfillment in Jesus would be shared through Jonathan's life and death.

A task that came easily for me was writing what I wanted to say to and about Jonathan. I knew him like no other person, I spent more time with him than anyone else. I knew what I had been focusing on teaching him and the girls.

Through tear-filled eyes, I penned the words that were in my heart, some words I wished I never had to say. My mind at times was still in denial of what had happened. But my heart knew without a doubt that things had been changed forever in an instant.

JONATHAN

Nicknames: Little Buddy, J, Buddy Rooskie, when talking about himself "Jone - Jonny," Captain Fat Belly

Favorite things: Looking for expensive cars while driving around, talking about Tesla's, googling for the biggest/tallest/oldest/most expensive things in the world, watching Marvel movies, Captain Underpants, wanting to play tackle football, playing games on mom's phone, playing with nerf guns, wanting an Apple Watch, Fitbit, a phone, negotiating to get what he wants, mommy and Buddy time, being mischievous, reciting movies, rolling on the floor with Charlie, eating nonstop, finding special rocks that he thought could be valuable like a diamond, always thinking about sharing with his friends and sisters, playing with the neighbors, trips to Ohio and Indiana.

Over the past week, we have talked about memories, watched the funniest videos, and browsed thousands of photos to remember and honor Jonathan's legacy. From the moment he was born, he was loved and adored by all who met him, especially his sisters.

Automatically, all the girls' friends adopted him as their brother; he was everybody's Little Buddy. We would joke that when he became a teenager, he would realize how lucky he was to be surrounded by all these older girls who adored him.

From early on, he had the privilege of being taken care of by Granmax, Grandma Cherry, Rach, Kimmy, Natalie, and Pilar, among others, who no doubt spoke vision and purpose over his life daily.

Many people would tell him to "give his mother a break," but there is nowhere else that I wanted him to be than right by my side, sleeping or awake.

CHAPTER 5

One of the significant traits he got from his dad is that there were always a million things going on in Jonathan's mind; not a minute went by that he was not replaying a movie in his head, and we would get snippets as he would randomly quote something.

We would all look at each other and laugh because it was so random to us at the time, and so impressive the memory he had for the things he cared about. He yearned to learn about the most significant, tallest, oldest, and most expensive things, and I enjoyed it when he shared that amazement and excitement with me. So many of our conversations started with, "Mom, did you know?" And ended with, "I learned it on one of my videos."

I had the privilege of getting to be called Mom and be the recipient of so much love, joy, excitement and adoration for all 9 years of Jonathan's life. One of my favorite things he would tell me is, "it's just mommy and Buddy time" and give me the sweetest look like he had been waiting for only that.

Jonathan's zeal for life was like no other; from early on, he would stay up late so he could spend extra time with me as I worked on things and was cleaning around the house. When his sisters were sleeping because they had to get up early for school, he would get his Mommy and me time.

On weekend mornings, I would find him up from bed early watching a movie or learning more seemingly random facts; he would tell me that sleeping was a waste of time. He would instead be seizing the day and finding funny ways to make people laugh or negotiating how to get a new game on my phone.

As much as Jonathan was loved, he was also very misunderstood. He would pace back and forth in his little *world, thinking about all the things and planning his next funny thing to say. He had so much wanting to come out from the inside of him that he couldn't sit still. Recently, I thought about how Jesus was found in the Temple, and he told his parents, "Don't you know that I should be about my father's work?" There were too many stories to tell, jokes to make, songs to dance to, Nutella sandwiches to eat, Teslas and Porsches to dream about, and nerf gun wars to plot, to sit still.*

I could see that God was going to use Jonathan in a mighty way. I tried to tell him as much as possible how smart he was, how much I loved him, that God loved him even more, and that God had a special plan just for him. I thought it would be by his sister's side in the J and K show, but God had a much bigger stage for him in heaven. I am so grateful for all the drives to and from school over the years with all 3 kids, especially recently when I was able to have conversations with Katie and J about life, God's word, and all the questions we all have, that only God has the answers to. So many times, we would just sing along to worship music together, declaring how great our God was.

In the last six months or so, J started sitting in the big service at Vous with me, and I'm so thankful for those times now. This led me to make sure that I was connecting with all three kids after service, we discussed the sermon and all the funny stories, and what they meant.

After Christmas, I downloaded a kids' Bible reading app, and I was so blessed that Jonathan would ask me to read it instead of playing a game or watching something. He enjoyed learning about God in each Bible story and, of course, had questions about why, how, and where.

Even more recently, Jonathan and I started a God and science devotional each night. It was the information that he craved, and he was learning how God orchestrat-

CHAPTER 5

ed and created all these amazing things. I will never forget how, for some reason, as soon as we started reading it, he had to read in another accent. Sometimes, it sounded Indian, British, and others were his made-up accents. This is what it sounded like in his very creative brain.

I looked forward to this time with him so much. Katie and I have continued reading it, and we feel close to Buddy. We know that he is asking all the questions and getting all the answers from the only one who has them.

Jonathan, I have so many questions that I will never fully understand. Why did God take you from us so soon? Did you fit your entire purpose into nine short years? I guess that's why you always tried to maximize each day.

When I feel sad, I remember all the loved ones who were with Jesus waiting to welcome you home: my dad, grandpa, and grandma Burke, Uncle Richard, and so many others. I know that your first question was most likely, "Do you have a Tesla here, and can I borrow your phone to play a game?"

Buddy, know that I will always miss you until the day we meet again. I hope that of all the things I tried to teach you, the most important was what Jesus did for us on the cross and how we can have eternal life.

I hope that when you met Jesus, you thought to yourself, "Mom was right."

> "I love you, Buddy. God loves you more. Sweet dreams, don't let the bedbugs bite. I won't see you in the morning, but I will hold you in my heart every day."

Everything that I shared about and to Jonathan is and was true that day. More recently, I have been thinking about some of the struggles that Jonathan was having at times in school as well. Those struggles have been private to our family, and I want to share them here with you because I have a new perspective on them.

Jonathan received detention twice for two different instances. In the first instance, he was very adamant with a little girl that she was not allowed to wear her sweatshirt because the teacher had told everyone to take them off. He decided he would help her by pulling on it a little to take it off. He should not be putting his hands on another person, so he received discipline from his school and us at home.

The other instance is when the kids were on the playground, and I don't remember the details of what they were arguing about, but Jonathan said to one of the other little boys that he was going to pull out a gun and shoot them. We were so shocked when we received a call from his school saying this, and obviously, this one brought even greater discipline. We had many discussions about where he had gotten those ideas, why he thought it was okay to say and what the results would be if he did that to someone—for them and for him. It was a chance to reteach the value of every life, how we do not have the right to react like that in anger, and how it was never ok to say those things or act on them.

This was also an opportunity to see what had been brewing in Jonathan's heart, to shed light on it before it had gotten to the point of genuinely causing harm to another person and himself. Ultimately, it was an opportunity to walk him through apologizing and repenting with those around him—the other students, teachers, and staff at school.

We wrote a letter to each family involved, and he stood in front of the class and apologized for his behavior, what he had said, and how he had scared the other students.

Most importantly, it was an opportunity to teach him how to go to his heavenly Father and repent of his sins because when we sin against others, we are sinning against God. We are all God's creation, and he loves all of us. He is always waiting with open arms. I am grateful for that opportunity to teach him the greatest gift that we can give our children, to run to Him in their time of need.

CHAPTER 5

After J's ceremony, fellowship time, and cleanup had ended; it was time to head home. Katie asked if I was going to ride with her; Anthony jumped in and said, *"No, Mom is going to ride home with me."* I felt so loved and protected at that moment, as if we had been genuinely united by this devastating experience. This was not always the experience of our relationship over the years, but we had turned a new leaf when we reunited the year before, and perhaps this would bring us even closer instead of tearing us apart. We talked about everything about the ceremony in the car, about how Pastor Rich Sr. had spoken to Anthony about being at a crossroads to run to God in this instant or continue to run away from him. Anthony's heart seemed more open than it had been in a long time towards God. My ultimate desire was for Anthony to be fully devoted and living for the Lord. Being united in the Lord in our marriage and family would give us a stronger foundation than ever before.

THE BURIAL

As we lay our heads to rest that night, we knew that we had the final step in this process—the official burial at the cemetery tomorrow. That would be a much smaller gathering of immediate family and very close friends. Our hearts and eyes would be faced with the agony of seeing the casket that held his body be lowered into the ground forever. The body that, at this point, I and the girls had seen for the last time 9 days prior. We had been given the option of going to the funeral home to say one last goodbye, but we opted not to; I don't think I could handle that. Anthony and his mom went, as she had not been here when they carried his body away from our house.

They requested any clothes that we wanted our loved one to be wearing and any of their things to be placed in the casket as well. We dressed him in one of his favorite superhero shirts and just underwear, which was quintessential Buddy attire. And at this moment, I don't remember if we placed anything else of significance in there. I think I cognitively realized that putting anything of importance there meant it would be gone forever.

Morning came, and it was time; the procedure of it was pretty quick. The pastor shared about our hope in Christ, the lowering of the casket, the tossing of the flowers, and the grief flowing over us once again. All the adrenaline, excitement of visitors, and planning of the last week had culminated in standing over a hole in the ground where hopes, dreams, and a part of my heart were now buried forever. At the house after, my sister's in-laws shared how their new grandson had just been born, and I had the horrible thought that came out of my mouth, *"One leaving and one arriving, the cycle of life."*

It was at the cemetery that my friend Natalie gave me the book by Levi Lusko, Through the Eyes of a Lion. That book would become a lifeline to me in the coming weeks, and every time I would read it over the years. It gave words to so many thoughts and feelings I was having and inspired me to voice and share them with the world, in hopes that I could offer the same to others on their grief journey. So would commence my journal entries that I would share on Instagram and eventually on my blog, and now in this book. A chronicling of the thoughts and feelings that needed to escape my mind, heart, and body. Otherwise, they would tear me apart and take me into deep despair.

CHAPTER 5

My prayer is that this book, my book, Forged by the Fire, will also be used by the Lord to help rescue you from the depths of despair. To be a metaphorical shoulder to cry on, the comfort of a warm hug, the refreshing shower to bring life back into your soul, to wash away the despair, even just for a moment. To be the voice of a friend encouraging you that you will be ok. You will rise above the waves of grief that often threaten to take you under, and through your life's journey with the Lord, you will be forged and refined by the fire, just as I am.

Scripture:
Isaiah 40:31, "but they who wait for the Lord shall renew their strength; they shall mount up with wings like eagles; they shall run and not be weary; they shall walk and not faint."

Prayer:
Lord, thank you for giving me unexplainable peace during this time and an extreme amount of faith in you, despite my circumstances. You were my strength, and I would have fallen and remained in despair if it hadn't been for you. Thank you for all the many blessings and miracles that happened and are still happening from Jonathan's story. Amen

Reflection Questions:
1. Were you able to praise and thank the Lord as you memorialized your child?
2. What was your experience with the cemetery and burial or cremation process?
3. Do you visit or reflect on their resting place?
4. Have you been honest with God about your feelings?

Here we are at the end of the saddest, darkest day section of my journey. These are the parts that are more structured and often visible to others. The next section will be less structured without any expectation of what does or doesn't need to happen. I permit you to fully embrace this season as well. Allow it to be exactly what you need it to be because each day is a new journey; a new opportunity to experience the Lord in the highs and the lows.

I have shared a few journal entries throughout the first few chapters of this book. The following section is a real-time unedited look at the outpouring of the highs and lows, the lies and truths, the questions, and the wrestling of my heart and mind that flowed out onto the pages. It is the intersection of the humanness of my existence, navigating the unthinkable, and the ultimate and everlasting goodness of God. I pray they will draw you closer to your heavenly Father in every way and increase your dependence and trust in Him like never before.

PART II: JOURNEY THROUGH GRIEF

THE HIGHS + LOWS

I lift my eyes to the hills - where does my help come from? My help comes from the LORD, the Maker of heaven and earth.
Psalm 121:1-2

CHAPTER 6

THE FIRST YEAR - 2020

February 24, 2020 - A Mother's Heart

I believe that just as God designed a mother's milk to change depending on what her baby needs, the same happens to her heart.

As her children age, her heart and her care change to provide them with the amount of protection and freedom to launch them into the world. When part of her heart is suddenly not needed anymore, that part dies.

The death of one of her children kills a part of her. I cannot heal my broken heart. Only Jehovah-Rapha, the God who heals, can do that.

"He heals the brokenhearted and bandages their wounds." Psalms 147:3

February 27, 2020 - Charlie

There are little things that bring me joy when I think about them, Jonathan being able to have Charlie is one of them. He loved him so much and was so excited when we got him. After saying good morning to me, Charlie was always next in line.

When we found Charlie, his name was originally Cyrus. I saw it as a sign from God that he was rebuilding our family, just as King Cyrus had instructed for the Temple of Jerusalem to be rebuilt.

We were coming off what at the time was our most challenging year as a family.

And now, in this season, I am holding on to God's promise that he will redeem and rebuild in His time. (Lord, please come back quickly)

> Looking back now it was only a training ground to exercise our faith.

Also, I have my times of getting pulled down in despair but thank you to all the friends and family who have been there to pull me back up, cry with me, give me space, remind me of God's promises, hold onto the memories, and hope for the future.

CHAPTER 6

February 29, 2020 - Blacker The Night

Today was a rough day...

Then I just came across a quote from a true story that I loved as a child, "The Hiding Place" by Corrie Ten Boom. She and her sister are in a concentration camp during WWII and are facing unimaginable horrors, but she writes this,

"But as the rest of the world grew stranger, one thing became increasingly clear. And that was the reason the two of us were here. Why others should suffer, we were not shown. As for us, from morning to lights out, whenever we were not in the ranks for roll call, our Bible was the center of an ever-widening circle of help and hope.

Like waifs clustered around a blazing fire, we gathered about it, holding out our hearts to its warmth and light. The blacker the night grew, the brighter and truer and more beautiful burned the word of God."

> Lord, please give me the strength to keep my eyes on you. Reveal to me the purpose even in my pain, and may I be a light to those in this dark world.

March 3, 2020 - Good Morning, Mom

No mother should have to visit her child's body here. It pains me to see his name displayed here.

No matter how many flowers we bring and how nicely they keep the ground, it doesn't change the fact of what this name plate represents.

I stood in the bathroom this morning and wished with all that I was that he would come bouncing in and tell me, "Good Morning, Mom", still rubbing sleep out of his eyes. He would hug me and ask if it was cold outside. I would tell him his clothes were lying on his bed, and then in would run Charlie.

Or as I was in the kitchen making lunches, Alayna would wake up J and K, then both of them would come say hi to me and hug me.

We were supposed to have so many more mornings together; I'm sure even on his last day of high school, I still would have been getting those good morning hugs. Believing that Jonathan is in the arms of Jesus is not the hard part; it's coming to grips with that he's no longer in mine that almost kills me.

CHAPTER 6

March 3, 2020 - This Is For You, Mom

"...difficulties and trials in life don't make us who we are; they reveal who we are. I believe they also reveal what we believe about God." - Jentezen Franklin

In the last year or so, every time something piqued my interest, whether political, theological, current events, family, etc., several different people and publications would start to talk about the same thing and help me investigate more or confirm my convictions. Someone would ask me about something, and I would have all the research ready for them.

"Right now, you are training for a trial you're not yet in. Public victory comes from private discipline." - Levi Lusko - Through the Eyes of a Lion.

In January, during a time of prayer and fasting, the Lord really spoke to me about praising God even when things do not go as I'm asking or think they should.

Every time I would see someone post how God wanted to bless you and expand your influence, etc.; which he does want to do for his glory. I would follow up with, "But even if he doesn't, I will praise him all the same." (If I only knew how much those words would be tested.

As Jonathan says in the video, "This is for you, Mom." Of course, when things are good, and you are maybe asking for a better job or another important but "trivial" situation, it's easy to say that you will praise Him no matter what.

"These things I have spoken to you, that in Me you may have peace. In the world you will have tribulation, but be of good cheer, I have overcome the world." John 16:33

> The true test comes when you are in the middle of your worst nightmare and can't breathe but manage to declare that God is good and that because of what he did for you on the cross to redeem you to himself, you have all you need.

March 7, 2020 - What Stage Are You In?

Yesterday, I had a counseling session to help process my grief; I was asked what "stage" I think I am at...

Truthfully, most days, if it were an option, I wouldn't leave my bed.

There is a permanent ache from walking through daily life.

My Little Buddy was by my side when I was not at work or sleeping. Where I went, he went. The constant reminders bring smiles and tears at the realization that those things are now memories.

Then there are the times when I hear of how Jonathan's life and my faith are impacting someone else's life, and for a small moment, I think that my pain is worth it and has meaning.

I see the new series starting at church on Sunday and marvel that months ago, when my pastors were seeking God, God knew exactly where I would be and needed to hear to feel that He is close and has not forgotten about me.

CHAPTER 6

Then, making plans for the girls' activities and thinking about where Jonathan is going to be. Only to remember, devastatingly, I don't have to worry about that anymore.

I saw a picture of him at school that his teacher printed for me and I thought to myself, "Of course, one of his shoelaces was untied."

Reading cards from his friends and seeing how special he was to each one and wondering how it can make any sense that none of us get to experience that special person any longer, breaks my heart.

I'm helping a friend with her daughter's birthday party, and the kids start watching old videos. Buddy runs in, and there's that pull again.

I'm going to dinner with dear friends and having a great time, but in the back of my mind, I am always thinking of the person who is no longer here with me. I'm smiling on the outside, but part of me is continuously dying on the inside.

As all over the place as this is, that's how my life feels right now. Before, I felt like as a family; we were walking through the different stages of each other's lives together, and now there is a big missing piece and several years of milestones, memories, hopes, and dreams that will never come to pass.

> Life having to keep moving is both a blessing and one of the hardest things I have to do each day.

March 10, 2020 - Your Burden - Your Blessing

It's been four weeks today—four weeks of feeling the deepest despair as well as the greatest outpouring of love and support.

"Your Burden is Your Blessing"-To Hell and Back, that's the series we started in church on Sunday. We're talking about Jesus' journey to the cross, his greatest burden, our greatest blessing.

Even in these past four weeks, I have seen God work in people's lives like never before. I have been given the chance to share the gospel with people I would never have had the chance to.

I have received testimonies that me being open about my journey through grief has helped others heal from past hurts, similar to mine or different. Several have donated to a cause in Jonathan's honor that will save preborn babies' lives. Parents have been given hope and the gift of life instead of death for their child and their soul.

I have compassion and empathy for those who hurt, which I have never had before. Even though I had valued the sanctity of life before, I now understand so much more about each person's spirit and how beautiful we are—beauty and value given to us by our Heavenly Father.

But still, there are times that I am angry and tell God that even with these amazing things he is doing through Jonathan's life and death, I would rather have him here with me. I long for his smile, his touch, his presence, and his special place in our family.

'Going a little farther, he [Jesus] fell with his face to the ground and prayed, "My Father, if it is possible,

CHAPTER 6

may this cup be taken from me. Yet not as I will, but as you will.'" Matthew 26:39

Lord, may I keep my eyes on the blessing I can be to others through my circumstances. May I focus on your blessing to us on the cross and the hope we have in you.

"A purpose-driven life is not a burden-free life, but because of Jesus, we don't carry the burdens on our own." Rich Wilkerson Jr.

March 11, 2020 - Heartbreaking Firsts

We donated a few things that I wish I could have back, but because we tend to store things randomly sometimes, I have been finding things here and there that help me breathe again.

> And even in these moments, God sends a word to tell me that he understands my pain.

Tonight, I found the clippings from Jonathan's first haircut. This picture is after, he was most likely eating an animal cracker.

As I showed it to Anthony, we did the little half smile/half cry and big sigh that has become customary when something reminds us of him.

The girls do it as well; it's a rush of 2 distinct emotions within a few seconds of each other. A rush of happiness to have found something that makes it feel like he's here, and then a rush of sadness, realizing it's only a memory.

Firsts have been very different now.

The first time I walked into his room, I knew that I would never be tucking him in again.

The first time I drove in the car, he wasn't behind me when I looked back.

The first time I made lunches for only the girls.

The first time I drove past his school, I didn't need to stop. Every day, I would text Katie, "Getting J now".

The first time I walked into church without him.

The first time I checked the girls' grades, he was no longer listed.

And so many other little firsts.

I long for the day when I can talk about the first time he runs into my arms again.

CHAPTER 6

March 11, 2020 - No More Seizures

I prayed that Jonathan's seizures would go away. That he would not have to be on medication anymore and would be able to play any sport he wanted. That I wouldn't have to tell him that he scared me last night because he had a seizure; thankfully for him, he never remembered them.

You could say that God answered my prayers.

As I sat with him after he passed, I told him I was sorry; I told him that I loved him, I told him to say hi to my dad for me, I told him I would see him again, and that he wasn't going to have any more seizures.

> What if your trial is an answer to your prayers? That's a hard pill to swallow.

This morning, I was listening to a podcast about grief by Phylicia Masonheimer. She was telling a story of a friend's baby who was sick and how they prayed for God to heal her.

She ended up going to be with the Lord, whole, and never to be sick again. So, even though their prayers were not answered as they wanted, God had answered their plea.

The hard part is suffering through the pain that we are still left with here on this earth. Guarding your heart so you do not fall into despair.

"Let the words of my mouth, and the meditation of my heart, be acceptable in thy sight, O LORD, my strength, and my redeemer." Psalm 19:14

March 13, 2020 - Look For The Helpers

"Every Little Thing Gonna Be Alright" - in the words of Bob Marley, Katie, and Jonathan.

And most importantly, GOD.

I lift my eyes to the hills—where does my help come from? My help comes from the LORD, the Maker of heaven and earth. Psalm 121:1-2.

Having someone close to you and part of your everyday life leave this earth changes how you see the world. You realize, like never before, how little control you have and how life is, as the Bible says, as a vapor.

It also brings into focus even more the sovereignty of God. Nothing on this earth happens without him knowing that it will. He is not surprised. Whether it be "natural" disasters, tragic events done by man, a death in your family, or a virus threatening to impact and possibly take several lives, he is not surprised.

And again, as he says in his word, He will work everything together for good to those that love Him and to glorify His name.

He will take what, at times, the devil meant to harm and will create opportunities for people to show love, compassion, and kindness. As they say during a tragedy, look for the helpers.

March 14, 2020 - I'm Just A Kid

I've been home today, cleaning with essential oils, tending to Katie because she's fighting a cold, and Alayna's tanning and cleaning out the pool.

I keep thinking of different things Buddy would be saying to me as I'm working around the house. "Mom, can I have a Nutella sandwich for lunch? And chips as my side? I had fruit this morning, oh come on Mom, I'm just a kid." He was such a little negotiator.

Alayna amusingly put Charlie on the paddleboard in the pool. Jonathan would really have loved to be in there with them. And then he would have run around playing ball with Charlie.

I found 2 of his Nerf guns out by the pool this morning. He loved those things and thought shooting his sisters was one of the best things in the world.

He would then be watching for the neighbors to come home, and as soon as they did, "Can I go see if the neighbors want to play? Come on, it's nice outside, and I don't have to do homework because it's pretty much like we don't have school for 14 days." Then he would tell me how spring break was on the 21st, but because of "the virus" (he would use air quotes), we had an extra week, and how this was the best day ever! I would, of course, bring him back to reality that he does have a little school this week.

He was constantly counting down and checking off how many days until various events, always looking forward to everything life had to offer.

I keep putting more pictures of him around the house. This kid had barely any pictures before (3rd child syndrome and bad decorator mom syndrome).

Now his face will be seen on almost every wall and table, possibly in every room.

CHAPTER 6

People remind me that I had nine wonderful years and 10 counting the time that it was really just him and me, with him in my tummy. But I long for so much more.

> This process is so hard, and sometimes the hurt almost outweighs the happy memories.

March 18, 2020 - You Alone Are My Heart's Desire

🎵 *As the deer panteth for the water*
So my soul longs after You
You alone are my heart's desire
And I long to worship You
You alone are my strength, my shield
To you alone may my spirit yield
You alone are my heart's desire
And I long to worship You 🎵

I've been pretty transparent about my journey and me holding on to faith even during my pain, but in the last few days, I have been even more challenged. Is it right that I long to go to heaven because Jonathan is there? Shouldn't I long more to go to heaven to be with Jesus and worship him?

Am I able to say, as Psalm 42:1 and this hymn say, "You alone are my heart's desire, and I long to worship You?"

I remember a few months ago, on the way to school, J, K, and I read about Abraham and Isaac and how he was asked by God to sacrifice his son. Abraham had complete faith that his job was obedience; everything else was up to God.

Today, I started to think about all the time that I would be having with Jonathan right now, with school being closed. I started again to think about the what ifs, blaming myself and others.

My focus started to move from a healthy state of missing him to doubting that God's will is supreme and that He is working on my behalf.

I have been asking God lately what it is that I need to learn during this time, because I don't want to miss this opportunity to grow, I don't want to wander around in this wilderness for 40 years.

> I think He is saying that He wants me to yearn for Him. Not to find fulfillment in myself, my marriage, or even my children, but in the Creator, the Alpha and Omega, the beginning and the end.

What a day it will be when we get to be face to face with our God to worship Him, and thanks be to our God that He supplied a way for families to be together again as well, if we choose to live our lives dedicated to Him.

March 20, 2020 - Becoming Normal Again

A lot of people are finding a new normal right now. It is almost comforting for everything to be not normal, because everything in my world was not normal after February 11th at 7 am.

The balance of a family is dependent on all its members. I notice it more now when one is missing than when each was added at birth. Being only a girl mom has felt strange because I know what it's like to parent both. (It's a good thing we have Charlie to add a little testosterone.)

CHAPTER 6

Carrying on with life as if nothing has changed is one of the hardest parts of losing someone. Going to work and trying to focus, interacting with people who may not know what has happened in your life, going to the grocery store and reaching out to grab an item but remembering that the person that loved that is no longer here, dishing dinner and stopping yourself from asking about that member of the family...

I know that the world is a place of extreme uncertainty right now, self-quarantining is difficult, and I would never wish for this turmoil, sickness and death on anyone; for me, it has been a blessing to have extra alone time to somehow become "normal" again.

March 26, 2020 - Grateful In Suffering

I am in a Bible reading FB group, and a couple of people are saying it is difficult to read the Book of Job right now because of the struggles everyone is going through.

Others encouraged them to keep reading to the end because God has the last word and He reveals His power, faithfulness, omniscience, and sovereignty in a big way.

And how beautiful is the deepened relationship Job has with God, as even through everyone and everything being stripped away in his life that he held dear, his praise to God did not waiver.

> I have tried to keep my focus on God's goodness and faithfulness, and I am grateful for so many things surrounding Jonathan's passing.

Such as, family and friends being able to travel freely to be with us from near and far. I can't imagine the added heartache of families not being able to grieve together right now.

My mother was close by and able to stay to help me physically and emotionally for several weeks.

My sister/brother-in-law and many others helped with the details of Jonathan's celebration.

Compassion and flexibility from my job.

Jonathan passed away at home, where I could sit with him right away and have privacy.

Friends who continue to check in and still send encouragement, love, and a listening ear.

A church family that continues to surround us now that our family is far away.

"The neighbors," who are family and loved Jonathan as their own, continue to help keep his memory alive and pull me out into the sunshine.

Being able to share the love and gift of Jesus in our lives. And countless other blessings.

May I be able to say as Job did, "You said, 'Listen now, and I will speak; I will question you, and you shall answer me.' My ears had heard of you, but now my eyes have seen you. Therefore, I despise myself and repent in dust and ashes." Job 42:4-6

CHAPTER 6

March 27, 2020 - Joy And Heartache

We spent the last few days painting a lot of the house as a family. A house that holds many wonderful memories as well as very heartbreaking ones. Thankfully, we have been able to smile throughout the tears.

For all the This Is Us fans: In the words of Dr. K, "I think the trick is not trying to keep the joys & the tragedies apart but you kind of got to let'em cozy up to one another, you know, let'em coexist...

and I think if u can do that, if u can manage to forge ahead w/all that joy & heartache mixed up together inside of you, never knowing which one's gonna get the upper hand... and well life does have a way of shaking out to be more beautiful than tragic."

And of course, most importantly, God's promise to us.

> "Being confident of this, that he who began a good work in you will carry it on to completion until the day of Christ Jesus." Philippians 1:6

March 29, 2020 - Jesus Strong And Kind

*🎼 Jesus said that if I thirst I should come to Him
No one else can satisfy I should come to Him
Jesus said If I am weak I should come to Him
No one else can be my strength I should come to Him
For the Lord is good and faithful
He will keep us day and night
We can always run to Jesus, Jesus strong and kind" 🎼*

Jonathan was always about the biggest, strongest, and oldest. He loved wearing this costume, and the date on it was February 17. I have no idea why he would be wearing a costume in February. I remember he loved putting his costumes on any chance he got, just like the girls and their princess dresses when they were little.

When I look at this picture, I think about how his muscles look big and strong, but they are full of fluff. They would never put up a good fight or hold up any real weight in a tragedy.

Over the last year, God has really been convicting me of having a strong biblical, theological foundation.

CHAPTER 6

I have sought out and found many resources that have helped me decipher between watered-down Christianity and verses used out of context to fit our situation or personal desires.

More recently, I have searched for worship songs that are focused on scripture and not emotion and theatrics. This song and group have been a great comfort, reminding me of Biblical truths and allowing me to focus on who God is, no matter my situation. I hope it can serve as a comfort to you as well.

March 31, 2020 - Hello Again, Tuesday Morning

Hello again, Tuesday morning.

Hello to all the images and panic of that Tuesday morning.

Hello to all the conversations about sharing the news that broke my heart over and over again.

Hello to all the love from friends and family who dropped what they were doing to run to my side.

Hello to the police officers, paramedics, and funeral home workers who showed care and kindness in the most difficult situations.

Hello to all the friendships rekindled and strengthened.

Hello to a special bond that the 4 of us share and to new memories.

Hello to all the endless conversations of God's goodness and never-ending faithfulness.

"The steadfast love of the Lord never ceases; his mercies never come to an end; they are new every morning; great is your faithfulness." Lamentations 3:22-23

April 1, 2020 - Do You Have Any Phobias?

Do you have any phobias?

Katelyn used to be so very afraid of heights, she wouldn't even like being thrown in the air.

Alayna told me today that she doesn't like small, enclosed spaces. She had a bad experience with one a few years ago.

Yesterday, we had our family counseling session via telehealth; she was telling us that we have to look at Jonathan and his life as someone who lived a full and happy 9 years of life, and not just someone who died.

CHAPTER 6

That may sound like a no-brainer for most, and it is what most people say to you to comfort you, but it is more complicated than you could imagine.

Shortly after, we were standing outside on the street with our neighbors discussing spiders.

It bubbled up inside of me, and with all the excitement as if Jonathan was standing next to me, I said, "Jonathan had arachnophobia; he would get so scared when he saw a little daddy long-legs."

We all laughed and carried on the conversation, telling stories of him and other things we were scared of.

> It was one of the first times that I discussed him and there was a genuine joy to share something about him. The ping of him not being there was just a little less.

Every moment is a journey, and of course, as I sit here typing, tears run down my face, but moments like that give me hope for the future.

April 7, 2020 - His Laugh, His Smile

Movies and TV shows have given us a false sense of the finality of death.

I would imagine that before "the entertainment age," it was easier to understand and accept that when a person was gone, they were not going to miraculously walk through the door.

But because of how emotionally attached we get to characters now, we mourn when they die, but they are brought back in memories or as a spirit still living within the story and experiencing life still with the family...or so many times, they were wrongfully thought to be dead and are still alive. So, mourning turns to rejoicing, and the pain does not last long.

I know those are fictional stories, but my mind has been made to believe that the actual reality of death is only for a short time, and Jonathan will miraculously run into my room and whisper in my ear ever so quietly, not to wake his dad.

Watching videos of him, especially in the last few months of his life, makes me question how he is not just on a trip to Ohio or Indiana, or just at school, waiting for me to pick him up.

I find myself smiling about him, his smile, his laugh, his jumping around, and everything else, but at some point, I always think to myself, "How is he not here anymore? How has he just gone? How is he so alive in this video, but now he's dead?"

Sometimes, it's hard for me to say that word; it makes it all too real.

April 10, 2020 - Happy Good Friday

Yesterday I was talking (texting) to a friend, and she asked if I treasure all the little memories more now, or if they have the opposite effect.

I told her, "I do treasure them. I wouldn't want it any other way. The joy will eventually outweigh the pain."

What a perfect picture of what we now call Good Friday. I can imagine how devastated Mary and all those who loved Jesus felt when they watched him be crucified on the cross. It *was their saddest, darkest day, but they had a promise to hold on to: Sunday was coming!*

Saturday must have felt like one of the longest days, waiting for the promise to be fulfilled. Each went through periods of denial, anger, feelings of sadness, bargaining, and depression, trying to cope in their way with what they were facing.

In the words of another great friend, "Even those who had lost hope and were hiding away in the upper room, fearing for their lives, were surprised by great joy on Sunday. I find that sometimes I can and do lose hope for periods, but God continually surprises me with joy that often follows my greatest storms."

Thank you, Lord, for the sacrifice of your son on our behalf. May I live each day to honor this sacrifice, holding on to your promise that even through our darkest days, you are risen and have overcome.

April 15, 2020 - First Walk Of This Season

Today, I took a walk. I left my house for the first time in five weeks, and longer than that because I barely left the house in February.

I walked in one direction so I could examine part of a dream and vision that God had placed in my heart.

The other direction I walked reminded me of a dream and vision that had died and been buried.

Every day, I live IN THE MIDDLE of these two places.

In the middle of heartache and hope.

In the middle of courage and discouragement. In the middle of promise and pain.

I am thankful for a God who meets me in the middle.

<u>April 16, 2020 - Little Special Moments</u>

Yesterday, Katie and I sorted Jonathan's cars; she acted out a scene from Cars and recreated a picture of the essential characters. Lol

I walked into my bathroom, and she was using my curling wand in her hair, so I helped her finish. We didn't spray them with anything, so they fell out pretty quickly when she went outside to play, but at least we have a picture. Anthony and I made dinner, and we all ate as a family.

And then watched Unstoppable, while Katie fell asleep on the couch. Alayna decided that midnight was a good time to start making a fantastic coffee cake, and we ate it at 2 am.

I know I often share the inspiration that's getting me through a difficult moment, or just my raw emotions.

CHAPTER 6

But know that, thankfully, I am not sitting in a corner all day. I am active in my life for maybe 85% of the time. (which is a lot more than a month ago)

> The little special moments get tucked away in my heart to help on days when those percentages may be a little different.

However, there's 15% of the time that often feels like I have to let something out or I will explode. This is usually what bubbles out onto the page. Thank you for your continued love and support.

April 24, 2020 - Sadness In Heaven

Disclaimer: I know all these questions are not theologically sound but stick with me until the end. (This is a glimpse into the mind of an analyzer.)

I have been wondering a lot about God's original plan for humanity. We couldn't just all live forever...could we? If we did die, would there be sadness felt by the people still living on earth?

If there wasn't sadness, would that be because there would still be some sort of interaction or communication?

And if there is no sadness in heaven, how is that possible when everyone doesn't go to heaven, if they don't choose to make Jesus the Lord of their life?

Wouldn't that make those in heaven sad, when all their loved ones are not there?

These are some of the thoughts going through my head when you see me staring off in the distance.

I'm not wondering what shoes are in style or what to make for dinner... just beginning and end-of-the-world questions, you know, normal everyday questions.

I think it's a way for me to try to escape my present reality and imagine another way that life could be.

I often have these anxious tendencies and thoughts. When this happens, I have come to realize that I/my situation is made to be the focus of my life or purpose.

Through reading scripture, I am reminded that this is God's story, and my part in it is to give Him glory. And scripture also brings me back to not worrying about the future but also not driving myself crazy worrying about the past.

> Instead, I want to live each day asking, "Lord, how can I help tell your story today?"

"I am the Alpha and the Omega, the first and the last, the beginning and the end." Revelation 22:13

CHAPTER 6

"Therefore, stop worrying about tomorrow because tomorrow will worry about itself. Each day has enough trouble of its own." Matthew 6:34

April 29, 2020 - Long Walks, Life + Government

Yesterday, Katie and I took a walk for an hour and a half. We talked about so many different things.

This was the first time that she had been outside our neighborhood since the quarantine started. She was very surprised to see how many people were out driving around and even walking or biking.

She said that she imagined empty streets because she thought everyone was at home.

(This is a whole other discussion on how our perception is often not reality, but that's for another time.)

Thankfully, we (especially the kids) have maintained a very active lifestyle, spending hours outside every day with our neighbors. However, we do live in a little bubble with no traffic unless you live on our street.

We made our way down to the cemetery and visited Buddy.

On my visits, I always think about how the grass that was dead on his gravesite is now getting green and how it is really so peaceful there. Of course, like many thoughts, I have never said these thoughts out loud.

But as we stood there, she said the exact words that I was thinking. How often do we feel isolated in our thoughts because we do not speak them out, even to God? (This is another discussion.)

I replied to her, "That's the cycle of life." What was once dead is now coming alive again. The dead grass breaks down and becomes part of the soil, helping to grow the new grass.

I started thinking about all the pain, regret, lost dreams, and heartache buried in countless graves, but sitting there, you get such a calm feeling. The grounds are beautiful, with lots of trees and wind chimes. We chose a section by a pond with turtles and fish that we visit each time.

This paints a very vivid picture of life to me. Even though we all have those feelings buried inside, we can look to Jesus and have peace beyond all understanding. We can flourish and thrive even while being filled with both death in certain areas and seeds that are growing.

"Forget the former things; do not dwell on the past. See, I am doing a new thing! Now it springs up; do you *not perceive it? I am making a way in the wilderness and streams in the wasteland." Isaiah 43:18-19*

This is a constant lesson that God is teaching me in so many facets of life, but as I reminded Katie yesterday, the light shines brighter because of the darkness. (This was during a discussion about politics and government; who would have thought?)

The joy is even sweeter because there was once only despair.

April 29, 2020 - Where Will Buddy Go?

Do you trust God with the big and small details of your life? Do you pray and ask him to direct you on what decisions to make?

Alayna was ready for high school, and Katie was heading into middle school.

We were leaving the school that all 3 of my kids had attended. Alayna, for the past 8 years. We were leaving a very close-knit family.

There were so many decisions to make, magnet school auditions, and applications. We were accepted and waitlisted at some schools. At the last minute, Alayna was miraculously accepted into her school because they "accidentally" sent her an email moving her off the waitlist.

> We decided where Katie would go to middle school for a theater magnet...so now we were left with one question...where is Buddy going to go?

It was too late to do any more school tours. I didn't know much about the school next to Katie's, but it was convenient and had a magnet program in 3rd grade.

Then God sent me an angel, Sherrie, to calm my nerves and show me where the right place was for Jonathan.

She was the costume designer at the school and highly recommended it and would put a good word in for Jonathan with the drama teacher.

Sherrie and I met 5 years earlier, in December 2013. I was selling Origami Owl jewelry and lockets, and she found me online. We have kept in touch over the years. She is a costume designer, and with the kids being in acting, we followed each other's journey.

My website name with Origami Owl was Celebrate and Inspire. It is a company that tells people's stories and has a focus on helping others. (The vision and

CHAPTER 6

purpose for the name are becoming increasingly clear.)

So, back to Buddy's school, it was May 18th, 2018, we were going to see the end-of-year show, Sherrie had gotten us free tickets because she wanted to show me what a fantastic drama program the school had. And help me to see that this was the right decision.

That night in the cast, a little girl, Gabi, was going to the same school as Katie the following year, according to the program flyer. Unbeknownst to anyone, Katie wondered all summer if she would be in her class and was very excited when she turned out to be in all her classes!

They have been best friends ever since; walking together through one of the most challenging seasons of Katie's life. Being there to laugh, cry, offer rides to and from school, and so many other moments in the last year and a half.

Katie walked into my room a few days ago and told me, "Gabi and I are going to do a Bible reading plan together". Nothing is sweeter to my ears, not only reading the Bible yourself but also making it the foundation of your friendship. And they are planning some exciting things with their other best friend, which you will hear about very soon.

So, long story short, we thought we were going to that show for Jonathan and my peace of mind for that season, but God's plan was much bigger.

It had started several years before, and He had several years ahead already planned, knowing precisely what we would need in this season.

No matter the circumstance, His ways are definitely greater than our ways. When you think about it, it gives a much deeper meaning to "not my will, but Your will be done." Luke 22:42

Will you pray to Him today and ask for His guidance? He wants to direct your steps and walk through every season with you.

May 1, 2020 - It's Gonna Be May

Last week, as I was adding our next family counseling session to the calendar for May 11, I noticed that the 10th was Mother's Day. I felt my heart sink. I felt all that heartache of one of my babies not being here to celebrate with me on that special day, and then the next day being 3 months since his passing.

I thought to myself, that's going to be a tough few days. I can picture myself not wanting to get out of bed, not because I'm working from bed, but because I don't want to face the reality that is my world. I let myself sit in that for a few minutes with tears rolling down my face. I shared my thoughts and feelings with Anthony, then I got up and told myself that I will get through it when it comes.

CHAPTER 6

There is no doubt that those days will be physically and emotionally difficult. But there are so many other days in the month that will signify celebration on this earth, and at this moment, I need to focus my time and energy on those to have enough joy to battle to the light at the end of the tunnel.

First, I have to celebrate the one and only Alayna Joy Simpson, who made me a mother. She was a surprise to me when I found out about her pending arrival, but she was loved and cherished from the very beginning. I know God was preparing her just for me.

I remember going home for lunch from work and thinking to myself, "Did I just pee myself?" Only to find out that my water broke, and she would make her entrance into our world later that night, May 25, 2004. Two weeks early but right on time.

> Born along with her and all God will do in her and through her, was a God dream that has been developing over the past almost 16 years now.

Little by little, I have gotten new details, revelations, and focuses, and have written them on the same paper. Adding updates along the way with the date so I can look back and see how God has been faithful.

Other celebrations:

In just a few days, it's my brother Simon's birthday

My niece Zoe's birthday is on the 17th, My father-in-law's birthday, Grandma Burke's birthday in heaven

2 good friends' birthdays and many others that Facebook will remind me about.

As well as celebrating my mother, grandmother, sister, and all the other mothers in my life.

And to finish out the month, the biggest kickoff to summer weekend, Memorial Day. We get to celebrate in remembrance of those who have given their lives in active military service for our freedoms.

So, in memory of my son, I will try my best to focus on celebrating all those I am still walking this life with, holding on to his memories while making new ones.

Come back to this post anytime you need to refocus; I know I will be a lot.

May 3, 2020 - This Day Over The Years

This day, 1 year ago, I wrote the post below.

"Do you look at the world around you and get lost in despair?

I do.

I often struggle with getting so depressed by the evil in the world that I feel bad about enjoying any good.

But I have to realize that we combat the bad by highlighting the good. We negate the hate by showing love. We heal the wounds by sharing hope. We silence our fears by being willing to fail because failure is progress. We celebrate light in a world of darkness by being the light.

This morning in the car, Jonathan was so happy it was Friday; he said that some days are not good. I told him that if he thought that, then they wouldn't be.

CHAPTER 6

Instead, we need to be looking for what we can learn that day, how to make the best of every situation, and how we can help someone else and make it a good day for them. That is how every day is a good day."

At the time of writing this post, I was heartbroken by all the pain I saw in the world. Our family was at a point of brokenness, in the midst of the most challenging year we had ever experienced, and I was reaching out to the only one who could give me peace.

We had started a new season. 5 months later, the ground was ripped out from underneath us.

Last October, our family was reunited. Almost exactly a year of being separated, we thought that we were out of the pit. We thought those bad days as a family were behind us.

Anthony and I were getting a strong foundation through a pre-marriage class at church, 15 years into our marriage, but better late than never, right?

In the Bible, Joseph faced many trials before he finally ended up in the palace. All seemed to be going well until he was confronted by Potipher's wife and wrongfully thrown in prison.

At that point, he could have said, "Today is a bad day." He could have said, "God has abandoned me."

He could have questioned all the dreams and visions that God had shown him.

Genesis 39:20: "...But while Joseph was there in the prison, the Lord was with him; he showed him kindness and granted him favor in the eyes of the prison warden."

Joseph stewarded the time and was faithful in the responsibilities given to him, never doubting that God would bring His promise to fruition.

So, my challenge today, in this season, remains the same as a year ago and all the years before this. How will I view each day? What will I focus on? Who will I look to for my help, peace, and comfort?

Today, "I lift my eyes to the mountains— where does my help come from? My help comes from the LORD, the Maker of heaven and earth. Psalm 121:1-2

May 11, 2020 - I'm Better At Writing

A few weeks ago, I was talking with a friend, and she told me that I should start speaking to groups about my process of grief and loss and how I've been able to hold on to my faith in God. My response was, "I've always been better at writing."

How often do we see in the Bible that different people try to tell God they aren't qualified because of an excuse? Something that they don't consider themselves talented at, or an insecurity or mistake that they want to hide?

None of us are qualified to do God's work; we can only submit to Him and ask him to use us. And when we ask God to use us, be ready to be uncomfortable.

So, on Friday, I was asked by a family friend if she could share one of my blog posts during her virtual house church Zoom. She added that if I wanted, I could speak as well. At first, I told her I would pray about which one she could share, as I was reading through them and seeking discernment, I kept getting this feeling like I needed to talk for myself.

CHAPTER 6

As I was praying about what to share, I realized that I could not discuss this season without mentioning other seasons in which God had been sowing and cultivating seeds in my life that have helped me navigate my current season.

I was vulnerable; I shared parts of my life that no one knew about unless they were present; I was transparent with my struggles and pouring out all parts of my heart to God.

On a rainy and cloudy day, filled with two sides of heartache and celebration. God knew I would need an extra push out of bed and gave me a purpose to talk about His love and faithfulness.

And as I mentioned yesterday, it is during my times of pain that I feel Him the closest, may I never forget that feeling and always yearn for Him to be this close.

June 21, 2020 - Father's Day

Grief is not something that you can choose or control. It is thrust upon you without your consent or regard for how it will affect every part of your life.

A global pandemic and lockdown are similar, as we have learned this year.

Less than a month after being thrust into this new journey of grief, we were all given a new set of rules to live by: 6 feet apart, mask and gloves, wash your hands, and groups smaller than 10 people...

> I already felt powerless over what had happened in my life, and now I was losing control over what I could do if I left my house.

So, I didn't leave. I stayed where I could control what I wore, how close I was to people, whether I wanted to sunbathe, and not just keep walking, etc. It was such a small amount of control I could still feel like I had.

I would tell people that I didn't want to go anywhere that I had to wear a mask, and they would say, It's just a mask. But it wasn't, and I might sound c r a z y, but it was another part of a decision in my life that was no longer my own. I needed to feel like I had some control, even though I knew I didn't.

I decided, through all of this, to get my wisdom teeth removed; might as well pour on the pain and hope that I'm good for at least the rest of 2020.

The experience was like no other, even though I've been through childbirth 3 times without any pain medication. But thankfully, my recovery has gone well with little pain after the first day. Thank God.

CHAPTER 6

One constant on this earth in our family through it all has been Anthony Simpson, from holding me up when I barely had the strength because my heart had been ripped out of my body.

To always trying to pull us together to watch movies as a family or play cards or scheduling our family counseling to ensure that we had different tools to work through this season individually and together.

Leading the way in our family renovations, against our opinions (which is why we now have a golf simulator in our living room), willingly doing all errands and grocery shopping because you didn't force me to face the world (and I know you like to be busy).

> Thank you for keeping our family going through it all, when we could have just shut down, you keep the girls excited about life.

Running back to Publix and Walgreens a million times for all the rare ingredients for Alayna's gourmet dishes, scouting out lychee and mangos, keeping the freezer stocked with every kind of Talenti flavor, except for the random weeks you decide you are on a diet. Lol

Making sure I have all my soft food options, making popcorn for movie nights, mango smoothies, omelets that I have to pick a million things out of, taking care of Charlie on early mornings when the girls and I sleep in.

And not to mention being the jack of all trades and fixing and solving all the issues and projects the girls and I come up with around the house (your screwdrivers are in the bathtub).

Thank you for finding strength for us all, even when at times you are fighting to find strength for yourself.

God chose you to be the father of our three wonderful children I know this season has brought you the most unexpected and heartbreaking experience as a father, but you have handled it with strength, love, vulnerability, and hope for the future of our family. Thank you.

July 30, 2020 - Facebook Grief Group

After Jonathan passed, I joined a grieving parents group on FB; losing a child is a very unique life experience, and I wanted the support from others who could relate but also wanted to be there to support when I felt led.

Life and this world can make you fall into despair in so many ways; it can be a rollercoaster of good days and bad days. The fight to get from the low of the bad days back up to the crest of a good day can often be impossible to muster in our strength.

CHAPTER 6

I thank God for his unchangeable, immovable, perfect comfort, strength, and peace.

Unlike the power of positive thinking, God comforts us in the reality of our situation and gives us the strength to hold on to his promises and the peace to know that he is in control, and we can trust Him.

"The Lord is my shepherd; I shall not want. He makes me lie down in green pastures. He leads me beside still waters. He restores my soul. He leads me in paths of righteousness for his name's sake.

Even though I walk through the valley of the shadow of death, I will fear no evil, for you are with me; your rod and your staff, they comfort me. You prepare a table before me in the presence of my enemies; you anoint my head with oil; my cup overflows.

Surely goodness and mercy shall follow me all the days of my life, and I shall dwell in the house of the Lord forever." Psalm 23

August 11, 2020 - 6 Months

Tonight, the girls and I read about redeeming the time, using our time wisely, and for the glory of God.

What have we done over the last 6 months since we lost our little Buddy? Have we wallowed in self-pity and sadness? Have we laughed even when we wanted to cry? Have we allowed ourselves to cry even when it felt like our hearts would explode? Have we wrestled with despair and hope; which one has come out on top? Have we heard the pitter-patter of his feet in the silence of the night?

Have we learned anything about the goodness of our God? Have we heard his laughter as something he found funny would come on, and it made us laugh and cry a little.

Have we remembered that because of the great love that was shared, there is immense pain in the loss? Do we want to mention him whenever we introduce the girls? Have we remembered to pray for those who mourn? Have we eliminated the idols that we had erected in our lives?

Have we remembered that God is faithful and sovereign, and no matter what happens in this life, He is our hope and comfort?

Some of those moments can drown out the voice of a faithful God. They can make us look to ourselves to put on a brave face and act like all is ok, and our world is not imploding. But God wants us to cry out to him, to let him into all the moments of our lives. He will comfort us and give us the strength to continue to pursue his purpose.

CHAPTER 6

God is not the god of name it and claim it, positive thinking, or come to Jesus and have a perfect life. But he is the God that promises to never leave us or forsake us, that he will sustain us if we are to truly love Him with all our hearts, and with all our souls, and with all our minds.

In the last 6 months, have we shared the Gospel, the only hope for a hurting world? Have we redeemed the time and drawn others closer to Him as we draw close to him?

> We live less than the time it takes to blink an eye if we measure our lives against eternity..."
> Chaim Potok

Because eternity depends on it.

"For God so loved the world, that he gave his only Son, that whoever believes in Him should not perish but have eternal life." John 3:16

September 16, 2020 - Blink Of An Eye

Last night, the flashbacks were like a waterfall, rehearsing that morning and the events of the rest of the day.

On the one hand, I am so thankful that I vividly remember that time. I never want to forget the last moments that we had with Jonathan's body as we fought to save his life. On the other hand, I felt the gut-wrenching feeling of not being successful, and everyone's reaction as they realized that this was not like other seizures he had before.

I wouldn't be able to talk to him and see him come back to me, let him rest, and then everything would be as if nothing had happened. I wouldn't be able to tell him that he scared me and get a hug and a sweet smile.

There wouldn't be a sweet smile this time.

As all the memories flooded my subconscious as I slept, they intersected with a dream of Buddy coming back to life and driving around with us, but things kept happening to the car; it wouldn't start, and then the wheel wouldn't turn, then we ran into a big puddle, and then he had a seizure in the car...what would happen this time?

> This night displays the roller coaster of life dealing with grief; some days are not the onslaught of memories and feelings, but some days are.

That's how grief is sometimes; we wish for things to be any way other than the tragedy that happened, thinking that life would be better, if only.

We torment ourselves with the what-ifs, but the what-ifs never end because they just lead to other what-ifs.

Every day, I try to remember Psalm 42:11,

> Why are you cast down, O my soul,
> And why are you in turmoil within me?
> Hope in God; for I shall again praise him,
> My salvation and my God.

October 8, 2020 - Identity

For over 16 years, I have identified myself as a mother of 1, 2, and then 3 children.

Many times, known as Alayna, Katelyn, or Jonathan's mom.

CHAPTER 6

Since 2010, I never imagined that I would walk into a room and be known as a mother of only 2 girls.

Even if the people in the room only knew me as Jonathan's mom, they most likely knew or had seen one or both of his sisters at some point.

But now, when I walk into a room, I am either known as a mother of 2 girls who is grieving her son, a mother of 2 girls because they don't know that Jonathan existed, or just me because they don't know anything at all about me.

But who am I now?

We so often identify by who we are married to, are mothers to, our job, ethnicity, gender, socioeconomic status, and so on. But what do all those things amount to?

Where or in whom do we find our identity? What do we idolize in our lives and think that it defines who we are and our value?

Soli Deo Gloria – Glory to God Alone

Lately, I have been wanting to define who I am to people that I meet for the first time but haven't quite figured out how to share Jonathan with strangers yet.

I am trying to submit this to God and desire to truly be known and held by Him.

> I've realized that it's a yearning for wanting to be known, to go below the surface and say that there is more than what you see or think you see.

When he looks at me, he doesn't see wife, mother, daughter, sister or friend as what defines me.

He sees the Imago Dei, made in the image of God.

He sees a life redeemed by the blood of Jesus and living through every season to give Him glory, no matter what that may look like.

October 27, 2020 - Sabbath

After coming back from our weekend away, reality and memories hit again once walking back into our house.

I had escaped the full effects for a short time, but the Lord reminded me that it is not in escaping during sabbath/vacation that will uphold me and carry me through, but the daily reliance and communion with Him.

May I nurture a consistent rest in you, Lord, appreciating and praising you for the beauty you created for us to enjoy. Dedicating all I am, all I have, and all I do to your glory.

CHAPTER 6

November 30, 2020 - What Gives Us This Confidence?

"You will be reunited again one day." "They are in a better place." "May they rest in peace."

All things that we say, Christian or not.

For a society that promotes living only for this life and denies the existence of God, a creator of all things or a greater power than ourselves, we are quick to comfort each other about peace in the "afterlife".

What gives us this confidence? What gives us this longing for more than the seen, the here and now?

In a conversation a few weeks ago, the person was saying that he is innately selfish; he needs to be given rules and told what to do. The truth is, we all are. But our depravity is so much worse than we realize. We are yearning for a creator to instruct us on how to live and how to have peace now and in the afterlife; something/someone greater than ourselves. We are searching for the meaning of life.

THE GOOD NEWS —
we were all created to bring God glory and to be in communion and fellowship with our creator forever.

But we chose to rebel, to not believe that God's way was best; we were separated from that communion, forever dead in our sin, condemned to eternal damnation.

BUT GOD, in His great mercy, made a way for us to be made alive in Him. To be reunited in fellowship with a holy God.

> Jesus came, lived a sinless life, died a death that we deserve, rose from the grave to conquer death, and established His kingdom. All for His glory and our redemption.

"For God so loved the world, that he gave his only Son, that whoever believes in him, shall not perish but have eternal life." John 3:16

THIS IS THAT CONFIDENCE - *this is what your soul is yearning for. In a relationship with your Heavenly Father, you are invited into His kingdom.*

*Put your trust in Him today, repent and turn from your sin against the Holy God, accept his gift of forgiveness and salvation, and ask Him to become the Lord of your life. *

No other message was more important to share at J's celebration of life or to use my voice to proclaim. We are not promised a perfect life, but we can live here and in eternity with our creator, if we accept His gift of salvation.

TURN AND BELIEVE TODAY.

CHAPTER 6

<u>December 8, 2020 - Confession Time</u>

For a few months after Jonathan's passing, it was hard for me to see happy families, especially with little boys. I would think to myself, "They have no idea how lucky they are."

Then I would pray that they never have to experience this type of pain. The other day in a FB grief group, someone mentioned that they don't even send Christmas cards because they can't bear to see all the happy families, when they have suffered such a great loss. I could relate to journeying through this feeling, but the Holy Spirit quickened this verse in my spirit,

"Rejoice with those who rejoice, weep with those who weep." Romans 12:15

Then I thought about all the pain and trials of people who have comforted me:

Years of infertility, treating my children as their own, while mourning in private.

Losing a 3-month-old baby, but never resenting Jonathan or our relationship, when their son would have been the same age.

Suffering a miscarriage and comforting me through their often-invisible pain.

This is a very small list of a few pains that are part of a great abyss that we do not see on the surface of happy family pictures.

But I was also reminded that the joy we see in family pictures is a very small glimpse of the everlasting joy awaiting us when we meet our savior in eternity.

> All the beauty in our world, the love we share with family and strangers, the joy of a baby being born, the innocent happiness of children laughing and playing, the display of bravery, courage and selfless sacrifice...

"So also you have sorrow now, but I will see you again, and your hearts will rejoice, and no one will take your joy away from you." John 16:22

"Every good and perfect gift is from above, coming down from the Father of the heavenly lights, who does not change like shifting shadows." James 1:17

I have started to pray a different prayer for those in a season of rejoicing and those in a season of mourning; that their joy may be made complete in the Lord.

"You make known to me the path of life; in your presence there is fullness of joy; at your right hand are pleasures forevermore." Psalm 16:11

CHAPTER 7

THE SECOND YEAR - 2021

January 15, 2021 - Coconut Water Companion

After a life-changing event, people and places sometimes have a crippling effect on you. The Holidays, they say, are the most difficult times, and you should prepare for them.

Prepare how you do or do not want to celebrate, where, what you will do when you need a break away, and how or if you will explain to others.

Many times, others will not understand your need for things to be a certain way because they need the opposite, or they don't even consider that this will be difficult for you.

You stress over it, come to terms with what will happen, and prepare your energy to endure. Soon I will share my journey through my birthday, Halloween, Jonathan's birthday, Thanksgiving, Christmas and New Years, that's exactly what it has been, a journey of mountains and valleys.

But there are always those unexpected places that have you breaking down in tears. Those places that you did not prepare all your strength for...

This time it was in the Target checkout line, somewhere that I hadn't frequented much because of the pandemic this last year but also hadn't really avoided either.

Jonathan loved coconut water; he knew I loved coconut water. As I saw the boxes of coconut water, I remembered how he would always work to convince me to buy it for him.

"Come on Mom, we can both share it, it's good for me, I know you love it, at least it's not soda. "

A little game of him convincing me to let him have what he wanted and him so proud of his accomplishment, but it really took no convincing me at all. (Don't tell him that)

He thought he was using his great negotiating skills and charm on me, and I loved that little smile he would give as he tried to sell me on a box of coco- nut water for the 2 of us.

"Mom, do you want another drink, or can I finish it?" He would always ask, such a gentleman.

As I stood there waiting in line, hiding behind my mask, I fought back the tears. Imagining that my little Buddy was next to me jumping around, holding his prized possession.

Alone with my thoughts, people all around but nobody seeing my pain.

Then it was my turn, and I was forced back into reality.

CHAPTER 7

Back to life without my jumping jellybean, coconut water companion.

January 29, 2021 - Home

Tonight, I went on a school tour with Katie, a school I had found last January for Buddy to go to. I knew that it would be a transition for him, but I know that it would have been the strong foundation and discipline that he needed to flourish and achieve with his best qualities.

As I sat there, hearing all the wonderful things about the school that I had fallen in love with the first time, I thought to myself, "Jonathan was supposed to go here, he should be here."

Then on the way home, as Katie and I were discussing different schools and options and seeking God for his will as to where she should go, I remembered that we are not made for this world.

I mourn for the loss of not seeing Jonathan grow and mature, but I forget that he is flourishing more now than he ever would on this earth. He was not made for this fallen world; he was made to have daily communion with his Heavenly Father.

Which he knows and experiences completely without stain or blemish.

The completion that we all yearn for.

As Christians we have to be reminded that this is not our home, our life here is to make Him known. To live in His will and to bring Him glory.

"So, we are always of good courage. We know that while we are at home in the body we are away from the Lord, for we walk by faith, not by sight. Yes, we are of good courage, and we would rather be away from the body and at home with the Lord. So, whether we are at home or away, we make it our aim to please him." 2 Corinthians 5:6-9

February 2, 2021 - Firsts And Lasts

This was an amazing day in downtown Miami with Alayna. We took the Metro, rode the loop, attended church in the park, walked around the city in the cool weather and finally decided on having pizza and wings. Kind of like we were in the Big Apple but with palm trees.

It was also Super Bowl Sunday in Miami, so the city was abuzz with excitement and tourists from all over the country. The perfect picture of a special day in more "normal" times.

Normal is a word we now use for pre - Covid, but for our family - normal - was a few weeks prior to Covid lockdowns. During the lockdowns, we would try to find our new normal. Such a blessing in disguise, I am thankful for small, unexpected mercies.

CHAPTER 7

Small mercies of not dropping Katie to school and passing Jonathan's, not making lunches for 2 instead of 3, not driving in the car and having an empty seat.

Having time to revamp the bedrooms and have bittersweet moments of it all being different but thankful that it was new, taking time to create family picture collages on our walls to keep the memories alive, time to walk to the cemetery and sit, cry, dream and pray, time to mourn with the world as life was changing for all of us, whether big or small.

Over the last almost year (just shy of 9 days), it has been a field of landmines of firsts just waiting to blow up in our faces. First Mother's Day, First Father's Day, First Birthdays, First Thanksgiving, First Christmas, First New Years and first every other day of the year that doesn't have a special celebration, only that Buddy is not present.

I feel like we have been climbing up this mountain leading to the unthinkable First 1-year anniversary...

His last 1st of the month, his last time eating pizza and watching a game of football with his dad, his last group photo, his last visit with his Grandpa and Granmax.

> Then yesterday the firsts stopped, and I realized that I would now be counting down Jonathan's lasts.

His last time at Alayna's swim meet, his last time complaining to me because he was bored waiting, his last full week of school, his last time practicing his lines with Katie for his school play, his last time at church, his last time looking for his shoes, his last homework packet, the last time I would wrap his cast *to take a bath, his last kiss goodnight and telling him "I love you."*

We had reached the peak and are now taking the rocky hike down the mountain and headed for the last of his firsts...his first day in heaven.

We will then start our journey through another year without our little Buddy, of which I'm sure will have its own highs and lows, one after the other until the day comes and I hear my Heavenly Father say, "Well done, good and faithful servant".

Until that day, I will keep my eyes on the One that is unchanging, immovable, and steadfast through each of life's trials and triumphs—in an ever-changing, anything-but-normal world.

Fear not, for I am with you; be not dismayed, for I am your God; I will strengthen you, I will help you, I will uphold you with my righteous right hand. Isaiah 41:10

CHAPTER 7

February 18, 2021 - Wholly Sanctified

"What's born in us through trials, through the pressure, is something so beautiful and new, something life-giving to the people around us. The Lord has birthed something new into the world through your character, the people you pour into, the people you disciple, the people you are able to impact.

The pressure brings forth life birthed in you and poured out onto others." - Phylicia Masonheimer

What a beautiful picture of how God uses everything for our good. How He redeems everything for His glory, if we will lay it at his feet.

We often think of "for our good" as prosperity, wealth or success.

What value are those things compared to knowing our Heavenly Father?

> What more do we desire? But to be wholly sanctified by the Lord.

To have wept at his feet, to have him carry you through life's storms. For him to use you to show his redemptive plan, for him to refine you by the fire?

"Now may the God of peace himself sanctify you completely and may your whole spirit and soul and body be kept blameless at the coming of our Lord Jesus Christ." 1 Thessalonians 5:23

March 10, 2021 - God's Faithfulness, Our Faithfulness

"I have learned that even though losing a child is a very unique pain, God expects the same faithfulness from us as in any other effect of this fallen world. So, the circumstances may be different, but we must lean on Him all the same."

I said this to a friend recently who called me for words of wisdom in a difficult situation. I was honored to be asked to share of God's faithfulness.

> ONE PROMISE—
> He will remain faithful to see us through to the end.

As I think of all the stories of God's faithfulness in the Bible—Joseph was sold into captivity, Abraham asked to sacrifice Issac, Esther living as an orphan, David attending sheep, Job lost everything and everyone, Daniel was in the Lion's den, Moses leading the Israelites, Noah building the Ark.

The New Testament apostles who were persecuted, jailed and martyred and so many others—all different

CHAPTER 7

situations, all different personalities, all different life experiences—ONE GOD.

Some looked for the Messiah to come, some walked with the Messiah, and like us, some had his written Word and the eyewitness testimony of others. There will be valleys, and there will be mountain tops, and there is no place I would rather be than in the arms of the One that holds the whole world in his hands.

It's hard to believe that these 2 pictures were taken a year apart. I can still feel the pit in my stomach as we went out to dinner for the first time. I cried in the bathroom stall before taking the picture, unsure of how to order food as if all was normal.

Putting a smile on our faces and all thinking the same thoughts but no one wanting to wallow and bring the other down.

Now, here we are a year later, a little wiser, a little more weathered with a little more patina around the edges, forever changed.

Behind these smiles is the faithfulness of God, the strength of a good father holding us up as we weather the storm, the promise of his presence forevermore and the bonds of love we share that can never be broken.

They say that hardship makes you stronger, but I think it's the foundation you stand on during those hardships and those you choose to tether yourself to, that keep you standing in the storm.

March 14, 2021 - Community

A few Sunday night thoughts that started out a little sad and turned into encouragement for myself and others.

"I miss the different relationships that form from having children of different ages, at different stages of life, and different genders. I used to have a place with the moms of elementary school kids and more specifically, boys. Now I'm just a teenage girl mom."

There is such a stigma of having children right now, that the world is somehow overpopulated. That each child is not a blessing and is born for a purpose at the time appointed by our Heavenly Father.

CHAPTER 7

All children may not be planned by us, as we are feeble, flawed humans, but they are all fearfully and wonderfully made.

I can clearly see why there is such an attack on the family, even in the body of Christ. Parents tend to gravitate towards those with children of similar ages, the family is a natural formation of relationships, a natural formation of community, a natural reflection of God's design.

My encouragement is to reach out to those at different stages of life, parents or nonparents. You may be able to support others, be supported, and create friendships that are a beautiful reflection of God's design instructed in Titus 2. Also, don't believe the lie that it is not a good time to have children, that the fewer children the better or that children are a nuisance.

Is having children always easy, no. But they are a beautiful way of being sanctified and growing in character and focus like nothing else can. They help expand your world, grow your empathy, and give you a chance to try to parent just a little better than your parents, and the cycle will continue.

For those who are not able to have children of your own, mentor the children around you. Parents need your wisdom and experiences; foster or adopt children in need or give resources to help where you can.

An extra bonus is that you can make friends with people at different stages, so your children and their lives will be enriched by it.

March 18, 2021 - Remember

> "Remember, you have your girls that need you."

Often said, trying to motivate someone to not fall into grief and stay there, to treasure what they still have after a loss or to bring some perspective to a dark and painful situation.

The truth is the loss of Jonathan made my job as a mother to my two girls even more important; it magnified that I was not promised tomorrow and to evaluate what I was doing to impact their eternity.

What was I teaching them by example, what Biblical truth was I searching out for them to learn that was being undermined in their everyday life?

Was I preparing them to live in a world of lies, was I fulfilling my job as a Christian parent or was I throwing my children to the wolves to be devoured?

We can't guarantee our children's salvation, no matter what they see portrayed or are taught.

CHAPTER 7

But it is my responsibility to teach them in the truth of God's word, equip them with the full armor of God, and pray that the Holy Spirit will open their eyes to see, their ears to hear and turn their hearts from a heart of stone to a heart of flesh, receiving Jesus as their Lord and Savior. (Jeremiah 31:33, Hebrews 8:10)

March 23, 2021 - Matured

A few nights ago, I said to Alayna, "Katie has matured like 4 years in the last year".

Then on Sunday, Pastor Jose was talking about Paul and the church of the Thessalonians, how Paul was encouraged and revived by them remaining in the faith, part of the church family. He understood that they were his crowning glory, he so loved the church family and knew that the future glory of heaven would be missing someone if they were not there, if they had not been steadfast.

He also gave an example from CS Lewis, in his book, The Four Loves, about his friends. Because Charles had died, there were now all these instances of Charles telling jokes and Ronald reacting to them that he would never get to enjoy. Now that Charles was gone a whole facet of Ronald's personality was gone as well, all the things that Charles had brought out and added to Ronald's life and therefore CS's life, were gone.

Katie and Jonathan were 2 peas in a pod, we always said that Jonathan was the boy version of Katie. He took her spontaneity, love of life and jokester personality to a whole new level. She was talented and organized and Buddy would just walk in and steal the show and only rehearse because Katie would have ensured he got some practice in ahead of time.

With Buddy gone, we are all missing parts of each other that Buddy brought out, and we can see parts missing in ourselves.

April 4, 2021 - What If I Didn't Do Enough?

> "You did everything you could, it was out of your control".

But what if I didn't...

What if I was randomly sent a letter to enter Jonathan into a sleep study years ago?

What if I knew I should have curbed his diet to nurture his brain better?

What if I talked many times about finding a more holistic neurologist to try different things?

What if I missed his appointment in December because of work and rescheduled and then missed that appointment because we were at urgent care for his arm?

CHAPTER 7

What if I was lax on his medication and had just started him on a new one a few months prior and should have been more on top of monitoring his seizures and their triggers?

What if we talked about getting more research done but didn't go the extra mile to get it done?

What if I heard a still small voice whisper, "seizure" to me as I was leaving his room that night, but I got distracted and didn't even check on him on my way to bed?

What if there are so many things about that weekend and years prior that haunt my thoughts and try to pull me into a drowning abyss of regret and sorrow?

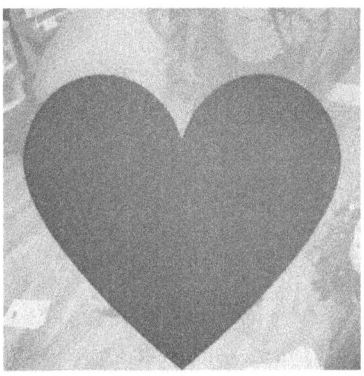

This is the last picture I took of Jonathan; I don't think anyone knows I have it unless they've seen it while randomly looking through my photos.

And now all of you do, but I still couldn't share the whole picture with you. I am thankful to have it, it's kind of that last look that people need to say goodbye. But at the same time, it haunts my dreams as I go back and look at it every so often.

Changing routine and coming back is hard, it's almost easier to not get a break from the even keel because then emotions flood back in and erupt (like this).

I can see why people move but that would be difficult to leave all the memories as well.

I don't have any wise words of wisdom; I think I am just overwhelmed with other decisions of life and feeling the ultimate pressure from my previous decisions.

I'm ok. This too shall pass.

July 25, 2021 - Endure

> The pain in giving birth is quickly forgotten because of the joy and love felt for the life that has been birthed.

A true gift from Heaven, which motivates us to endure it, again and again.

I've never heard the pain of death explained in the same way.

However, as time passes, I realize that the pain of loss rushes in and for a moment you feel like you cannot endure or overcome it.

But thankfully the sharpest pain does not last forever, and the joy of life pushes you to endure day after day.

October 22, 2021 - The Wall

This wall was installed when we painted the house and refreshed J and Katie's bedroom last year. It has been an outlet for different thoughts and has served many purposes—notes to and from friends, notes to

CHAPTER 7

Heaven, school presentations, summer activity wish lists, and most recently, a collection of quotes and catchphrases from favorite movies and shows.

As I sat here and looked at it the other day, I realized that's how our minds work and look. A collection of what phases we are in and focusing on, a plethora of different messages bombarding us directly and subliminally.

I decided that I wanted to use it to display scripture verses, promises that would ground Katie and soothe her soul as she walked past it, lay in her bed or chose a necklace or outfit to wear.

I wondered if I should erase everything else but realized that reading scripture or posting it on our wall doesn't immediately erase all the other thoughts in our head—it shouldn't and doesn't need to.

His promises that have been imprinted on our hearts and hidden deep down in our soul, will last forever

But over time, those promises will become more prominent to us. When we look at the wall, we will focus on the scripture, everything else will fade and rub off over time.

"For the word of God is living and active, sharper than any two-edged sword, piercing to the division of soul and of spirit, of joints and of marrow, and discerning the thoughts and intentions of the heart." Hebrews 4:12

December 17, 2021 - Gravestone

Little Buddy finally has a marker for his earthly resting place.

When we visit the cemetery, the girls and I often walk around and look at other markers and remark, "Oh this person was young or elderly, this person must have been a mother or it was their birthday recently, etc."

I hope that when people look at Buddy's they see the love we shared and the joy he brought to our lives.

CHAPTER 8

THE THIRD YEAR - 2022

January 6, 2022 - Gray

Do you ever cry out to the Lord honestly without holding back?

In the middle of November, I wrote the below post but did not share it publicly, however I wept to God as I wrote it. Just a few days later different things started to happen to move things from the gray area to more black and white.

Am I happy with the direction that each circumstance is heading? Absolutely not. But am I grateful that the Lord heard my pleas, cares for my heart and has said that He will carry me through, no matter where the road may lead? Absolutely Yes.

"How long, O Lord? Will you forget me forever? How long will you hide your face from me? How long must I take counsel in my soul and have sorrow in my heart all day? How long shall my enemy be exalted over me?

Consider and answer me, O Lord my God; light up my eyes, lest I sleep the sleep of death, lest my enemy say,

"I have prevailed over him," lest my foes rejoice because I am shaken. But I have trusted in your steadfast love; my heart shall rejoice in your salvation. I will sing to the Lord, because he has dealt bountifully with me." Psalm 13:1-6

> Losing Jonathan was a full stop, admittedly the hardest journey to walk through but I knew where the road ended. It ended with Jonathan in heaven and me still walking this earth.

This current season has been much different; it has been a never-ending roundabout with possible exits or different roadways that could open to different avenues to the rest of my life.

Everyday waking up wondering how this will end, what am I praying for in this situation, should I be retreating or pursuing?

I don't do well in between, or gray areas. I am very much a black and white type of person.

Throw in Jonathan's headstone still not being done and all the emotions of having to even order and design that, raising 2 teenage girls who are 1 minute my best friends because I see some of my best qualities in them.

Then the next minute, I feel like I'm failing in every way possible because I see how they could make my every mistake as well. And in my deepest desire to push them toward the Lord, am I actually pushing them away because of how imperfectly I try to guide them?

CHAPTER 8

February 11, 2022 - 2 Years

I was in the bathroom getting ready, Anthony was downstairs in the kitchen, and the girls were just getting up for the day.

I can still hear and feel the events of that morning. I can feel the anguish and despair that flooded our home in a single moment. I can remember texting my mom and sister, "Please pray".

Please pray for the unthinkable to not be happening. Please pray for a miracle. Please pray that the Lord would intervene and reverse anything that had already happened.

But those prayers were not answered in the way we desired. We were thrust into the unthinkable, we did not get our miracle. Jonathan had already left this life and was in eternity.

Today is 2 years since that day. 2 years of longing, 2 years of praying for the Lord to return so that we can be reunited. 2 years of people witnessing our perseverance and sharing how they have also persevered, and in return, strengthening our perseverance.

Yesterday we had a donut picnic at the cemetery and ate way too many in Buddy's honor. Anthony brought his favorite Tesla and we read from his favorite devotional. It's about the greatness of God in His creation. J would always say, "How Greeeeat!", like Tony the Tiger.

The one we randomly read was about Isaiah 43:19, "Behold, I am doing a new thing; now it springs forth, do you not perceive it? I will make a way in the wilderness and rivers in the desert."

This verse does not pretend away the desert and wilderness but gives us the promise that the Lord will be with us in them. Even there, he will bring forth new life, living waters. All is not dry and desolate; He will make a way and strengthen us.

As we enter year 3 of life without Buddy by our side, may we hold fast to the Lord that never leaves or forsakes us. May we perceive all the new life and where He is leading us. And may we depend on the Rivers of Living Water to sustain us.

Love you, Little Buddy, and will miss you every moment of every day until we are together again.

CHAPTER 8

February 21, 2022 - Moving

The girls and I are moving.

Anthony already moved out last August.

I could tell you how I felt abandoned, rejected, worthless, heartbroken, devastated, angry, and without hope at times, even now. I could tell you how I failed many times to not sin in my anger, about all the resentment and bitterness that was growing inside of me — and I will one day. (my book is getting longer and longer)

But I'd rather tell you about the lessons I hope I have exemplified and shared with my girls, the deep work the Lord is doing to sanctify and purify me and how the Gospel has become even more real to me through this situation.

Do I pray for reconciliation? Everyday. Because I truly believe that God's best design is for 2 to be joined in covenant for life and that will always take hard work and sacrifice of ourselves, which is a small imperfect glimpse of the gospel and in this the Lord is glorified.

> But I have come to realize that the redemption of all things that God promises does not always equal reconciliation in this life.

If I were to believe that God's purpose can only be fulfilled if we feeble humans follow His best/His commands perfectly, then how have I limited God to be at the will and command of our decisions?

I serve a God that is sovereign over all and works everything for my ultimate spiritual good and His glory. And only He knows the beginning from the end.

I pray that in my own life and the life of our family, my girls have seen firsthand that our decisions all throughout life have consequences and that others are affected by those decisions. But also, that no decision that we make is outside of the forgiveness and sovereignty of our great God.

That everyone (including myself) will at some point disappoint or hurt you. Let this push you into the arms of the One that will never leave or forsake you; His love never fails.

Anthony may have made the ultimate decision to walk out but in God's eyes, every time I turned my back instead of showing grace and love, every time I focused only on my needs instead of those of my husband, I was walking out too.

But God in His great mercy paid the price for all my sins on the cross, all I have to do is repent and accept His forgiveness. I pray that Anthony comes to this conviction one day and surrenders to Jesus as his Lord and Savior. And if we never spend another day together in covenant on this earth; I pray we spend eternity worshiping together.

Does this take away the pain? No. Will I most likely cry as I take down the last of our family pictures? Probably. Marriage and family are 2 of the most sacred things to God and when it dies, there should be and is a grieving process.

I am thankful to forever be part of the family of God, the bride of Christ. His love is everlasting, steadfast, loyal and He paid the ultimate sacrifice with his life to show us this love.

CHAPTER 8

He has worked on our behalf to ultimately redeem all things and reconcile us to Himself, our greatest reward.

And Yes, even in the midst of everything, the Lord has been good in so many ways. And He will continue to be.

April 9, 2022 - Unholiest Labor

What has been your "unholiest labor," as Jordan Lee Dooley puts it?

What have you strived for, believed God for, been faithful in (admittedly insufficiently and imperfectly) and in the end it seems that all the laboring was for nothing? That all that striving only led ultimately to heartbreak anyway?

All the years of lessons, of hardship, loss and suffering, of believing that my decisions led me here and I was going to try to reflect and portray to my children, the example of a Godly, committed, flawed but faithful wife.

Only in the end to be faced with the hardening of my husband's heart that never softened truly toward our commitment and ultimately toward the Lord in submission.

Why do the trials, hardships and suffering of the last 18 years not warrant a testimony of reconciliation and the goodness of God?

Why like in Egypt, did God not soften Pharaoh's heart, but it says He actually hardened it? Why couldn't he have humbled him to fall to his knees and together we be an example of God's great power?

Why instead do I have to feel his rejection of me and my Lord over and over? Why has my unholiest labor seemed to only serve the purpose of bringing me to my knees in submission to a holy God?

May 8, 2022 - Sole Protector And Provider

This is me at 8 yrs. old, sitting at my dad's gravestone. I've been thinking about the ripple effects from this moment in time. One of the greatest being that my mother would now carry the mantle of "sole protector and provider" of me and my siblings. A job she was never meant to bear alone or at all.

CHAPTER 8

As I would see my mother imperfectly fill this role, as any human can and as my father also would have, so would start my search for someone to make me feel protected and provided for—like only One can.

My mother would never be able to protect me from the hurt of this life, the struggles we went through or the longing this world could never satisfy.

In the same way I would never be able to do any of these things for my children. No matter how much I try to keep them in a bubble, shield them from my own inadequacy, or save them from going on this same search for earthly protection and provision, my only hope is in pointing them to the One; it is there that I will continually find Him too.

Of all the things my mother did or didn't do, the most important happened at 5:30 every morning. Before the day began, before her own fears and inadequacies crept in. Before each of our searches continued, she searched the heart of the One she prayed we would one day find too.

May my children also say this of me, that in all my strengths or weaknesses, apparent success or blatant failure and in my own search in this life; that I have found the One, "The Sole Protector and Provider" - Jehovah Jireh.

And my mother's heart prays that in all their searching; they will find Him too.

June 24, 2022 - The Night Before

February 10, 2020

That was the last time Katie sat at this piano.

June 22, 2022 - the day we returned

As we drove into the neighborhood, we commented on how grown and full the trees looked (as does Katie now too). The street had a different feel to it, and we actually pulled into the wrong driveway trying to find our way back to what used to be on auto pilot.

As we walked up to knock on (the right) door, Katie commented on how long it had been...almost 2 1/2 years. She said she shouldn't have waited so long to start again or shouldn't have stopped, I said "that's ok, life has seasons."

> Some seasons are about surviving, fighting to stay afloat, some you start to heal and some you find your way back to something that will help you heal even more.

And many times, all those seasons are happening in all different areas of life, all at the same time. Once the door opened, it was like we had never left.

The hugs were like a warm blanket and a testament to say that we had survived, we were still here, and we had returned with fresh passion and motivation to develop and grow.

This season may feel different; we may take a couple of wrong turns as we try to find our way, but we will continue to knock and know that the ultimate RIGHT DOOR will always open.

CHAPTER 8

"Ask, and it will be given to you; seek, and you will find; knock, and it will be opened to you. For everyone who asks receives, and the one who seeks finds, and to the one who knocks, it will be opened." Matthew 7:7-8

September 13, 2022 - Beauty In Pruning

As I came downstairs, I noticed the stillness of the water and the perfect reflection of the trees and sky.

The bushes/tall grass was not something I focused on. I had seen them before, and I take notice of them more when they have dragonflies and butterflies bouncing off their tips and fluttering to and fro.

A few hours later I could hear the maintenance of the grounds outside my apartment. Nothing out of the ordinary, until I saw the beautiful bushes. The dragonfly playground had been pruned and cut almost to the ground.

If this had been my first time seeing them, I would not have thought anything of it because I wouldn't have known the beauty that had been there before. I would only know what my eyes now beheld.

In knowing both the beauty and the stages of pruning, I know the beauty that is to come.

I know the growth that will be gradual and beautiful to witness, I know the smile that will fill my heart and face as I see the long stalks reach toward the sky and sunshine and I know the dragonflies will return.

But even now, I can see into the depths of the bushes, nothing is hidden, nothing obstructing my view of the lake and the banking.

A beauty to behold of its own. And I realize that there is beauty in the pruning, the growing, and the flourishing; we just have to rest in the season that we are in.

September 25, 2022 - Heaven Rules

At Jonathan's funeral, we sang, "You're a good Father," and shared the Gospel with all who attended, young and old.

On the morning of February 11th, 2020, the devil thought he had won. The devil thought that all the seeds of faith that had been sown would be ripped out of the ground in an instant.

We had bright balloons and smiling pictures of a short life here on earth. We wore superhero shirts, knowing who was the ultimate greatest Hero.

We listened to Vika as she sang about our healing coming through tears and what if our biggest disappointment or the aching of this

CHAPTER 8

life is the revealing of a greater thirst this world can't satisfy.

We didn't curse God and say, "How could He have allowed this to happen?". We didn't allow our pain to push us permanently into despair and run from the only One that can rescue us.

He thought the death of Jonathan's earthly body would be the death of us all.

But God had another move. God used February 11th to shine a beacon of light from the hurting of this world to the hope of heaven.

On February 19th, He delivered a blow to the enemy as what was supposed to crush us instead made us sing of His goodness even louder.

What was supposed to turn us inward, instead turned us upward.

We could sing of everlasting hope in a moment of deep despair because—HEAVEN RULES.

"They will make war on the Lamb, and the Lamb will conquer them, for he is Lord of Lords and King of

kings, and those with him are called and chosen and faithful." Revelation 17:14

October 8, 2022 - 40th Birthday

"You don't look like what you have been through." - my friend

Me: "Because the God in me is bigger than any circumstance!"

A lot of my life I was constantly looking back and searching for what was the missing piece. Once identified, I would go into self-pity and what ifs. A different life with my dad still alive, a different personality, a different set of talents or passions, different life choices and spouse...different struggles and challenges.

I would wear a mask, pretending like all was well, that I was just this way and harp on all that I had been deprived of.

CHAPTER 8

Meanwhile searching for something to fill the void I felt but not expressing to anyone the deep hurt.

The healing started about 4 years ago and was sent into hyper speed after losing Jonathan. The ultimate hurt was on display for the world, and this hurt would have ripped me apart if I wasn't able to cry out to God in honesty and share with friends and family to help us all address the hurt, we had buried and tried to cover.

Once I reached my point of complete reliance on God, he began to put my parts back together. Turning all my yearning for acceptance and security into an identity firmly planted in who I was as His daughter.

No more hiding or blaming my circumstances or living in the what ifs.

Each day laying down my thoughts and feelings and reminding myself of who I am in Him. Crying out to him and thanking him for those he has placed in my life to help hold me up and push me forward, as I do the same for them.

Instead, it turned to, "Lord everything belongs to you, you have allowed all things to bring about your great purpose. Heal me and expose what needs to be pruned. Sanctify me for the road ahead, use me for your glory."

This 40th birthday is for all of us, the Lord has sustained us and fortified us, and He will never let us down!

"No, in all these things we are more than conquerors through him who loved us. For I am sure that neither death nor life, nor angels nor rulers, nor things present nor things to come, nor powers, nor height nor depth, nor anything else in all creation, will be able to

separate us from the love of God in Christ Jesus our Lord." Romans 8:37-39

December 19, 2022 - Memories

"Learning how to hold things close and cherish them but completely release them to the Lord at the same time."

At Christmas, we celebrate the physical birth of our King, the coming of our Messiah—whose life and death would give us freedom from sin and welcome us into His eternal family. A family that will never be broken by loss or pain but an everlasting promise,

"So then you are no longer strangers and aliens, but you are fellow citizens with the saints and members of the household of God," Ephesians 2:19

In celebrating our savior, we extend that celebration to the physical family he has given us on this earth. The people we are bonded to thru Storge - the kind of easy bond that naturally forms between parents and

CHAPTER 8

their children and sometimes between siblings in the same household.

Unlike our eternal family that we are grafted into as Christians when we believe that Jesus is who he says he is— that he is fully God and man, that he lived a sinless life, died for our sins, and rose from the dead. When we submit to him as Lord of our life and live to glorify him in all we do...there is a bond that will never be broken...

The pain and brokenness of this world often mars the celebration of our earthly family, we lose parts of our family and ourselves that leaves holes and longings for those we no longer are able to walk this life with.

For each of us, we continue on this road in our unique way. Some remember only in their own hearts all the special memories they have, and others need to/like to have a visual reminder; something that draws their heart to that memory and gives others a glimpse into times and people they may not have had the privilege to know.

The circumstances do not have to be a physical death, it could also be a divorce, a new marriage, estrangement of a child or moving to a new area. Loss comes in many different forms and affects each person involved, differently.

> This Christmas season, remember the greatest gift of Jesus and the eternal family the Father wants to welcome us into. Cherish the blessings and the lessons in your own unique way and allow others to share in the memories with you.

December 28, 2022 - Podcast Launch

Today is the 28th of December (I know you're thinking...why yes, it is lol). Well today represents many things and it officially now represents...

THE CELEBRATE + INSPIRE LIFE PODCAST LAUNCH DAY!!!

It has been in the works for a while now and I keep going back and forth on where I want to take it, don't have an official plan laid out and no fancy equipment...but a friend told me to push record and start the podcast...so here I am!

All I have is a heart dedicated to the Lord, and if even one person comes to know the Lord or deepens their dependence on Him from hearing my voice, then His purpose for them will be fulfilled, and that's enough for me.

But here I am, taking 1 step and trusting the Lord to lead me to the next one.

> To be honest with you, I woke up anxious as I am being faced with moving again, it's a symbolic day, that time of the month and I started to feel like what's the point, no one will listen anyway...

Episode 1 will be out tomorrow, and we will discuss in more detail what today has represented in years past, the inspiration of my podcast cover and ebenezers in my life of God's faithfulness. As well as a hint where next week's episode will broadcast from.

CHAPTER 8

Thank you for walking this journey with me as we Celebrate the Lord's faithfulness in every season and area of life + Inspire you to seek Him, the giver of Life, in stewarding all He has given you and in pursuing all He has for you to do in building His Kingdom.

December 29, 2022 - Ebenezers

Yesterday was December 28th, you are probably saying to yourself..." Why yes it was." Well yesterday would have been my 19th wedding Anniversary, and I knew that significance was pushing me even more to announce and launch my podcast on this day. Kind of a way to redeem the day from always thinking about what could have been or what was, but also holding the day for new birth, a fresh start, a new journey.

So next year on this day, I will think to myself, this would have been my 20th wedding anniversary; as I always, even in a small way, will mourn that loss. But I will also think to myself, this is the 1-year anniversary of launching my podcast, launching a new way for me to spread my testimony of the faithfulness of God. Who was with me for all 20 of the prior years and will always be with me in the future. A promise that I will take any opportunity to remind myself and those within an earshot of.

So now going back to the pictures on my original cover art, the picture that you see of me was taken in the cemetery when I visited Jonathan on his last birthday on November 23, 2022. For those that are new on this journey,

> I was surrounded by all the memories of these loved ones, including my own, all these dreams that had ended too early, all the sadness and loss but at the same time, such beauty.

Jonathan passed away on February 11, 2020, at the age of 9, so he would have been 12 on his birthday this year.

I was sitting there quietly and noticed how beautiful the sunset was and how it was shining through the trees nearby. It was truly a golden hour as they call it.

The gravestones that signify the beginning and ending of a physical life on this earth are stagnant, but everything around me in this life continues and signifies that we had survived, I had survived.

So, I took a picture with Buddy (his pictures on his gravestone at least) and took one of just myself. Because I wanted something to remind me that I was not buried in that ground with him, the sun was still rising and setting on my days, I still had work to do. The Giver of Life was sustaining me to go on.

As I stated in the trailer and could easily quote each episode, Isaiah 41:10, "Fear not, for I am with you; be not dismayed, for I am your God; I will strengthen you,

CHAPTER 8

I will help you, I will uphold you with my righteous right hand."

The other picture is of my favorite plant in my room (don't tell my other plants that). This plant sits in the corner that doesn't get direct sunlight and when I moved it into my room, I thought it may not thrive because of this. But as I saw this plant start to thrive and grow new leaves, I realized that it was getting sunlight from the mirror that was reflecting the light from across the room.

This illustration again highlights how we can be going through a dark time in our life, where we feel like we are hidden from the light. Maybe we have even experienced death and feel like we are dying. This plant looked like it was dying before I brought it into my room.

> When we read God's word, pray and fellowship with other believers, then the light of Christ is reflected into our hearts and lives. We are reminded of His promises even if our circumstances may not change.

And at the same time, as Christians we are reflectors of His light, we shine his light into our dark world.

Matthew 5:14 states, "You are the light of the world and it gives light for all who are in the house."

In the world, we reveal the good and the bad according to God's law (because He is holy, the King of kings and Lord of lords), we explain why there is all the darkness (because of the Fall of man that brought sin into the world) and we explain who created the beauty (the Lord) and lastly we offer clarity and hope in the darkness (because we are proclaimers of the Gospel, the good news).

We are the light because we are one with Jesus who says in John 8:12, "I am the light of the world. Whoever follows me will not walk in darkness but will have the light of life." We have the Holy Spirit, so have the same light as Jesus and through sanctification will walk in the fruit of the Spirit.

> Both of these pictures serve as Ebenezers for me, a moment to look back on and be reminded of God's goodness and faithfulness. Even in my darkest times, he was carrying me through, shining his light, giving me life and sustaining me. He is worthy of all the glory for all my days.

my plant and the mirror reflecting the light from the sun, we as Christians shine the light of Christ in this dark world. We reveal where there may be disease or decay and provide nourishment needed to grow and thrive eternally (because of the hope of Christ and his work on the cross).

So, a challenge to all of us as Christians, are we reflecting/shining this light? (Imperfectly of course) Pray to the Holy Spirit to give you grace, love, compassion and passion to shine His light and the opportunities to do so.

CHAPTER 9

THE FOURTH AND FIFTH YEAR
2023 + 2024

February 21, 2023 - 3 Years

It's crazy to think how three years have already passed, that's 1/3 of the time that I had Jonathan on this earth with me. In those three years, I now have an adult daughter, another daughter that will be touring colleges next year, I am officially the status of single on every form I fill out, and the gray hairs are becoming increasingly abundant.

I've said it before, but life continuing is a blessing and one of the hardest things after such a loss. You want to continue with life because you want to see more beauty, and to see those that are still here create a life of their own. We want to celebrate with them but at the same time, the further down the road of life that you travel, the less and less there is of the one that you lost.

Recently, with what happened with my brother and his heart; during the nine minutes that they were giving him cpr. I was taken back to that morning when

Anthony was giving Jonathan cpr. The 911 operator was giving him instructions over the phone and paramedics took over, but J was already in heaven

And then last night after Katie and her little cousins were done watching Madagascar two, one of J's favorite movies, the song "move it move it" was playing.

I could see Jonathan dancing to that song and shaking his little booty. So again, it's a blessing and one of the hardest things to have your memories because just as you remember the good times, the bad times are even sometimes more distinct and real when you remember them.

> Last night at dinner, Zoe commented on how my table could fit all my kids and me, if Jonathan were here, Rachel replied how he is always here in our hearts.

Zoe also asked me for a new Jonathan bookmark, we gave bookmarks out with John 3:16 at his celebration of life, because hers is so worn out from all the use.

Life can feel like that sometimes, worn out from all the use, not always from bad stuff because using a bookmark means that you are reading and learning and, in this case, getting a reminder of a loved one each time you use it.

I had a thought this morning, maybe we should laminate Zoe's bookmark of Jonathan, that way it won't get worn out. It will stand the test of time, marking exciting journeys in the pages of a book, if it falls to the floor and gets stepped on or if it falls in water, it will not be changed.

CHAPTER 9

How do we laminate our own lives? How will we stand the test of time, the exciting journeys and the times when we feel downtrodden and overwhelmed by the waves?

This can only be done by grounding ourselves in the word of God, placing our identity and foundation in Him. Knowing his character, promises and how the story ends, with him returning as victor. This will fortify us and, in the times, when there are happy and sad, we know that we can take both to him and he will carry us.

I pray friends that this truth becomes more real to you than anything else in this world, that you place your trust in Him and his everlasting goodness. And no matter where life takes you, what you accomplish or what or who you lose along the way, that you will surrender to the Giver of eternal life. Putting your trust in Him and his goodness.

February 16, 2023 - Wait Go Trust

Are you seeing what the Lord is doing? Are you waiting with expectation?

Are you moving with those following the voice of the Lord?

Are you trusting His timing? Sometimes that means going alone.

Are you keeping your eyes on the vision, the destination?

Sometimes you can't see all the details, but you trust the One taking you there.

When I talk to people about specifically the last few years, I can see how gracious the Lord has been to me and my family. How he has been kind to nurture and provide for me in each situation and transition.

Each season has been hard in its own way, but I can see how it happening in a different order; it could have been so much harder.

The Lord reunited Anthony and I a few months before J's passing, we were more focused as a family than we had ever been.

Experiencing such a loss, made the transition of our family and Alayna going to college more palpable due to all He had carried me through already.

I can't imagine going through that loss without him there to lean on and grieving as a family.

The Lord's kindness in this last year gave me respite from the world around me, an oasis of calm where I could bask in his creation every day.

CHAPTER 9

And now moving into a new season, he has given me calm and peace and has expanded my vision even further. In conversation a couple nights ago, I was asked what my plan for the future is...I said, "Well in a couple years Katie will be in college and who knows where I will be...maybe off on the mission field somewhere."

In the last few days, I have felt a big release to further let go of physical items. The Lord knew that I needed time to cherish the memories those items hold; to make new memories with them and see how gently he is moving me into a new season.

I am ready to follow your voice Lord, send me.

"but they who wait for the Lord shall renew their strength; they shall mount up with wings like eagles; they shall run and not be weary; they shall walk and not faint." Isaiah 40:31

March 23, 2023 - Feb + March

Today 6 years ago we were on our way to Jamaica for a wedding and then we moved into the best neighborhood a week later; where we met the best neighbors who are now family.

3 years ago, a few weeks ago, my life changed forever.

1 year ago, I had just moved into this apartment, a few weeks ago.

This year, a few weeks ago, may symbolize another big change we will see in the future.

And this Saturday I am moving again.

February/March has become a pivotal time in my life, my growth and the direction my life is headed.

I have shed a lot of material, physical things over the past couple years and even more emotionally. This has been freeing and scary at the same time.

> May I always look to the Lord for where He is leading and trust Him to carry me through the next season.

I can't wait to see where the Lord will stretch and grow me, how he will expand my love and dependence on Him and how He will prove himself faithful. Let's go!

September 27, 2023 - Puzzles

As far back as I can remember, making puzzles has always been special to our family. An often group activity that requires no talking but naturally fosters communication, stimulates the brain, offers calm relaxation, and you are free to come and go as you need or linger as long as you like. Easy, non-competitive bonding and building of core memories.

What do you think keeps us coming back time and time again?

Is it taking what seems like a million (more like 1000) pieces all broken apart and meticulously figuring out how each piece creates a beautiful masterpiece?

Is it that thrill you feel when you find a piece that fits and the motivation to find the next one and the next one that keeps you at the table or on the floor for hours?

CHAPTER 9

Is it sometimes looking for a specific color or shape and getting the surprise that a completely unexpected piece actually fits because the colors look different before piecing it all together?

Is it how, as you get into the more complicated of puzzles, the pieces don't always really interlock perfectly; sometimes they just rest on the side of each other, and another piece has to connect them to each other?

Is it that feeling of excitement of piecing the unique, somewhat random pieces together and how you can look at the same pieces for hours when suddenly one jumps out at you, and you realize you had overlooked it all this time?

One of the hardest parts is when a puzzle piece gets lost along the way; you never quite have that satisfaction of completeness.

What about the accomplishment you feel for a short time after finding that last piece, and then it quickly fades into...

"What puzzle are we going to do next?"

> Puzzles apparently are a lot like life, before laboring for hours, days and sometimes weeks; there was a creator that printed the puzzle, cut each piece and knows exactly how each will fit back together.

Do we trust Him to cut and divide?

Do we trust Him and continue searching for Him?

Because He is the only missing piece that will truly bring us lasting satisfaction.

April 23, 2024 - 4 Years

I was in Italy on a beautiful, sunny day fellowshipping with a lovely family of believers who so graciously opened their home to us. It had completely slipped my mind that it was Feb 11th. 4 years to the day of my son Jonathan, passing away. How could I have been so distracted that I was oblivious to this anniversary?

It was such a blessing to be traveling on this day and enjoying this new experience but in an instant, all of the grief and regret and sorrow hit my body and mind, and I began to sob uncontrollably.

> I also felt guilty that I was not with either of my girls on that day, if I couldn't be with Jonathan, then I should be with my other children if possible.

I realized at that moment that we often dread these days as they arrive each year but also the days and weeks leading up to them is a time for our body to prepare, for us to work through the emotions that this day will bring and to commemorate it how we wish.

CHAPTER 9

But when we do not take that time, no matter how extensive, the shock of the day can sometimes hit you like a fresh wound reopened.

The Lord used this time to minister to my heart, thru Sister Esther, Robert and also the church family from Italy.

It was a raw outpouring of the real unfiltered emotions of the memory of that day and a sweet demonstration of us receiving comfort and others being comforted, by seeing us be comforted and His faithfulness to sustain us.

And in the ways the Lord revealed my pain and grief, He used it to bond us together and open the door for me to offer comfort to another mother grieving the loss of her son in different ways, even though he had not passed from this earth.

Oftentimes we think we have nothing to offer, but we underestimate what sitting and listening, praying, crying, saying I see your pain and so does God and you are loved, does for another person.

When we look at the life of Jesus, we see that this describes most of His ministry. He sat, he ate, he cried with people over the pain in this world, he called people to lay down their burdens and their vices and follow Him, he offered to carry their burdens for them.

He never acted like they didn't exist, he said I know you cannot carry this alone because you were never meant to. And paying the ultimate price with his life, he took on himself not only the temporary pains we endure in this life but the eternal weight of our sin that requires judgment by a holy God.

He has endured the ultimate pain, the ultimate grief, the ultimate separation from the Father, so we don't have to, if we only believe and surrender.

I am eternally grateful for this trip and all that the Lord did and is continuing to reveal to me. I pray that it is the first of many opportunities to unite with the hearts of brothers and sisters around the world, holding on to the savior and living their lives to proclaim His glory.

Just as all creation, cultures, tribes and tongues of every part of this earth declares the glory of our great God. We are so privileged to be allowed to play a small part.

From my heart to yours, dear friends, I pray that you have received comfort from the Lord and encouragement to persevere with hope.

February 11, 2025 - From Death To Life

Today is 5 years since my greatest test became my greatest testimony.

Over the weekend I was given the opportunity to speak of God's faithfulness during a time that could have brought me down into despair and kept me there. In preparation I knew that it was the faithfulness of the Lord over my lifetime that had built my trust and faith in Him. I saw how those seeds of faith planted early in my childhood had grown and bore fruit in its season. Just as the Lord promises.

The truth of God's love and Him being a good Father has always been my anchor. Knowing that this was never God's original plan; He didn't want his children to suffer. I am thankful for his redemptive plan in

CHAPTER 9

sending Jesus and one day He will wipe away every tear.

The Lord also invited me to publicly lay everything down before him once again and arise from the water with renewed consecration and fortitude.

I did not go into the weekend or that morning planning to be baptized but the Lord knew all along what He had prepared.

It just so happened, which we know wasn't a coincidence at all, that the shirt I was wearing was the shirt from J's celebration of life. Blanca (and another friend) had made it for us, Simpson party of 4. And now as my pastor, she was baptizing me in it 5 years later.

Certain dates are significant to me, for obvious reasons and I was originally planning to release the cover of my book today, to signify a celebration on this date. Turns out I don't have much of a voice today and couldn't talk about it anyway.

But we have so much to celebrate; the Lord did a work in me over this weekend that went way below the cov-

er, the surface, and allowed me to be used by Him in others' lives as well.

I will continue to hold fast to the promise that He works everything together for my good and His glory. He is writing His story, and I have the privilege and the honor of being part of it.

> I love and miss you always, Jonathan, and I dream of the day I will see you again. In the meantime, we have a lot of work to do together.

CHAPTER 9

Friends, we have walked through quite a journey of discovery together, and I know that we are each most likely at different points in our individual journeys. Thank you for joining me for a part of mine and allowing me to be a part of yours. For some of you, the wound of your broken heart is very fresh, and you are gasping for air and strength to stand.

Others are a little further along and have—through the help of others, allowing the Lord to carry them, and with the gift of time, become accustomed to this new version of themselves and their heart.

The patina that has formed on you or them is a beautiful reflection of the weathering that happens over time and how it draws out more beauty. No matter where you find yourself on your journey, the Lord is walking every step with you.

In this last section, I provide you with practical next steps on your healing journey. You can scan them and see what is most helpful to you at this time, read through them and discover something new or store them away for the future. Please don't feel pressure to dive into everything at once or feel less than if you need to just close this section of the book and come back at a later time. My prayer is that these pages can be a source of connection, encouragement, and support for you in your time of need, whenever that may be. Or maybe you will be able to share them with a friend or family member. I know the Lord will use this entire book how He has destined for it to be used. His message of love, redemption, healing and purpose will reach all who He has ordained for it to.

As you lean into knowing Him, His truths and promises will become the wind beneath your wings and will propel you into your purpose, as you take one step at a time.

PART III: JOURNEY TO HEALING

And after you have suffered a little while, the God of all grace, who has called you to his eternal glory in Christ, will himself restore, confirm, strengthen, and establish you.
1 Peter 5:10

CHAPTER 10

THE GRACE OF LAMENT

As I have had the privilege of sitting and hearing stories of other's journeys, I clearly see the grace that has been given to me by the Lord. A grace to fully trust him and lead others to see the goodness of the Lord even in their journey through grief. I want to invite you into a different type of grace that I have discovered in a deeper way recently, something even deeper than the journey through grief. I want to invite you into the Grace of Lament. This is what Mark Vroegop calls it in his book, "Dark Clouds, Deep Mercy"; which I will be sharing thoughts from.

My friend Brittany gave me this book shortly after Jonathan passed away. I will admit that I did not read it until just recently and I don't really know why I delayed, but I believe it was a gift that the Lord had for me to discover at precisely this very moment. I have been praying to the Lord and asking him to grow my compassion for mothers who are questioning the goodness of God, are angry at God, or mothers having a difficult time accepting the new reality of their child no longer walking this life with them.

I know that what I learned through the grace of lament is a gift that is applicable to everyone who journeys through grief, and now I have the privilege of being used by the Lord to help reveal it to you as well. Vroegop says, "to cry is human, but to lament is Christian." Lament invites us to grieve and trust, to struggle and believe. It is a prayer in pain that leads to trust, it is God's given alternative of silent bitterness, despair or denial, vain hopes and unpacified confusion.

Looking back, I see that I lamented more as I went through my divorce as that was a time that I felt all my efforts, prayers and perceived 2nd chances had all been in vain. You may remember that I wrote a journal entry on April 9, 2022, titled, Unholiest Labor.

This was a term I learnt from author, Jordan Lee Dooley, in her book, Embrace Your Almost. I verbally asked God why I had to keep feeling the rejection of my husband over and over. Why did the trials, hardships and suffering of 18 years not warrant a testimony of reconciliation? Why had I not seen the goodness of God, but this had only served to bring me to my knees in submission? I was heartbroken and I was angry at God because I felt like he had failed me. He allowed His goodness to be displayed in my life differently than how I thought it should.

Maybe this is how you are feeling about the loss of your child, like it is your unholiest labor. Lament welcomes us to ask questions that are not always accepted, especially in our Christian environments. *"Where are you, God?"* and *"If you love me, why is this happening?"* are two that we can start with. I'm sure we could both come up with more questions, and I welcome you to voice them or write them down. Let them pour out of your deepest hurt and wrestling and flow up to the throne of your heavenly Father.

We see in the Psalms that David regularly laments with the Lord; Vroegop identifies that biblical lament tends to include four key elements:

- Address to God - choosing to pray instead of resigning to silence

- Complaint - boldly but humbly explaining to God the situation that causes our suffering

- Request - bold request based on God's character

- Expression of trust and/or praise - actively waiting on Him and remembering God's deeds of salvation through Jesus and through our years of walking with Him

CHAPTER 10

In a one-word summary - lament is to turn, complain, ask, and trust.

It is not often that we see someone encouraging us to complain to God. I don't know that I came humbly with my complaints as I lamented. My rage was self-centered as my expectations had been crushed; they were not God-centered. I possibly even felt that since I had been faithful all those years in my marriage and had endured the loss of my son, then why should I be asked to endure the pain of divorce and betrayal as well?

Our complaints instead are to come out of a heart that desires to see the distance between God's promises and our painful reality being abridged. A desire to bring heaven to earth and an outpouring of not currently seeing that reality in our circumstances.

Before you start complaining, be sure you've checked your arrogance at the door. Come with your pain, not your pride. This was something that pierced my heart; it reminded me of when God asked Job, *"Where was he when He laid the foundations of the earth?"* God understands that in our humanness, we are in great pain, but just as our children should still come with respect in their pain, so should we when approaching the Lord. I see this also when the Bible tells us not to sin in our anger.

If you don't have the words, just open the Psalms and read one. Psalm 13 is a good one to pour out your soul and allow it to open your heart to the Lord.

> How long, O Lord? Will you forget me forever?
> How long will you hide your face from me?
> How long must I take counsel in my soul?
> And have sorrow in my heart all day?
> How long shall my enemy be exalted over me?
> Consider and answer me, O Lord my God;
> light up my eyes, lest I sleep the sleep of death,
> lest my enemy say, "I have prevailed over him,"
> Lest my foes rejoice because I am shaken.
> But I have trusted in your steadfast love;
> My heart shall rejoice in your salvation.
> I will sing to the Lord, because he has dealt with me bountifully.

Remind the Lord of His promises and of His faithfulness and remember that this also grieves His heart. We know that his character does not desire to see His children in pain, so He sent His only son as a sacrifice to redeem all things and one day, He will dry every tear.

Be honest with God about your fears and pains, remember that God is not surprised, Christ empathizes, and the Spirit intercedes for us. The things that break the Father's heart should also break ours, share those things with Him.

Seek to move forward with God. Bring him into every tear, every heartache, every moment of despair, every question and every complaint. Don't leave him out of anything. Through the tears the first step is to turn to Him in prayer, not away from him.

Following complaints, we move into asking boldly. Vroegop contends that God's people are, in fact, commanded to ask boldly. Hebrews 4:16 states, "Let us therefore come boldly unto the throne of grace, that we may obtain mercy, and find grace to help in time of need."

In the lament Psalms, there are nine petitions or requests for lamenting people. *"Arise, O LORD!"; "Grant us help"; "Remember your covenant"; "Let justice be done"; "Don't remember our sins"; "Restore us!"; "Don't be silent – listen to me"; "Teach me" during my pain; "Vindicate me!".* As we pray these prayers, we are called to trust that "songs of sorrow and the Man of Sorrows meet us in our pain. They invite us to move from why to who by calling upon God to act.

That's why asking boldly should finally lead us to trusting God. This reminds me of when Jesus asks Peter in John 6:67- 68, "Do you want to go away as well?" Simon Peter replied, "Lord, to whom shall we go? You have the words of eternal life". We complain to the Lord because He is our ultimate comforter; we boldly ask of Him because we know He is the only one who can grant our requests, and we fully trust Him because we know He is working everything together for our good.

In this turning of our heart, we choose to remember God's saving love in many ways, but ultimately, we go to the gospel where his steadfast love shines the brightest. Trusting in God's promises does "not end the pain, but they do give it purpose." And in trusting God, although the pain might not end, it "becomes a platform for worship".

CHAPTER 10

These words from Vroegop remind me of what has anchored me in my journey, "The loss and death of my son was never God's original plan; he never wanted me or you to suffer in this way. He wanted us to enjoy fellowship with him for all eternity, without pain or the tainting of sin that we experience in this world through death. And I am so thankful for His redemptive plan to use/redeem all things together for our good and His glory if only we would believe in Him and love Him Romans 8:28."

This revelation, promise, and hope grounded in God's character was a gift to me that was unwrapped as I searched my heart on that fateful morning. The question was posed to me, "Will you leave me because of this?" My answer could only be, *"Who else will save me from this, and who has made the ultimate sacrifice? Where else would I go?"*

My invitation to you is to embrace the gift and grace of lament. Turn and address God in your pain; do not turn away from Him. Bring your humble, honest complaints to him and allow Him to grieve alongside you. Boldly request of Him all he has promised in His word and all the attributes of His character. Trust Him and express to Him your praise. Come with a thankful heart and praise Him for how He has been faithful and for His salvation of all that you are and ever will be.

Regardless of where you are in your journey through grief, I pray that you find yourself accepting Vroegop's invitation to lament and, "Keep trusting the one who keeps you trusting".

CHAPTER 11

SOUL CARE

FALLEN INTO DESPAIR

I remember that first night trying to go to sleep. I remember how a lot of the day was a rollercoaster of my stomach feeling like it was leaving my body because of all the emotions rushing through it and my heart breaking into a million pieces over and over again. When night came, that was a whole different story; I shared about it earlier in this book. All the adrenaline and love and doing everything to put one foot in front of the other comes to a crashing halt when your body stops moving. Where are all those emotions and all that adrenaline supposed to go now? Where is all the love that was helping me cope and continue throughout the day? Whenever I close my eyes, will my mind always be searching for evidence that this is just a nightmare? Will the flashbacks always haunt me? Will I feel like I can breathe again, or will I suffocate in my tears? Will my body always feel like my heart is being ripped out of my chest?

Will I always feel so weak but also can't stop moving in bed because my body won't settle down? Friend, do you still feel like what I described above? Does it feel like it is still that first day or night? Do you struggle to just get out of bed in the morning? Do you struggle to sleep because of flashbacks? Do you feel like you don't know your body anymore because there is forever a missing piece, and now you have disassociated from your body? Do you neglect to take care of yourself or your family and other children?

Have you not been able to look at their things, talk about them, or have relationships with people connected to them? Are you not able to focus, be creative, or show up at work? Do you find it difficult to find joy or happiness in anything in life? Have you considered that it would be better if you were no longer here?

What other ways would you describe how you are going through life? Are you like a zombie? Or do you mask it so well that no one would ever know? Does everything come crashing down again when you are alone?

Are you scared to share those thoughts and feelings with anyone for fear of being judged or have you shared and regretted it? Have you sought professional help and nothing has helped?

We were never meant to try to survive this, to continue living after losing part of our actual body, mind, and heart. It's ok and normal for this to be our reaction. The hard part is often knowing, "Where do we go from here"?

The first thing I want to tell you is that if this is you, the Bible talks about how the Good Shepherd leaves the 99 and goes and seeks out the one that's hurting and in danger. He does not desire that any perish, eternally or in this present life. So, know that He has not forgotten about you; you are not a random person in a crowd of people. He knows you and loves you, and the very fact that you are reading this book is a testament to that.

You were the one for whom I wrote this book. The Lord wants you to know that He will never leave you or forsake you, and He has sent people to walk alongside you and help hold you up. You are not a burden, and as others help you regain your strength and purpose in life; you will then be able to do the same for others.

During Elijah's time hiding in the wilderness, he falls into deep depression and expresses a desire to die. 1 Kings 19:4 "But he himself went a day's journey into the wilderness. He came to a broom bush, sat down under it, and prayed that he might die. 'I have had enough, Lord,' he said" If this has been your prayer, you are not alone. You are not broken or failing for feeling like this; cry out to the Lord. Pour your heart out to him, truly lament, and don't hold anything back.

CHAPTER 11

Please reach out to me on Instagram or join our Celebrate and Inspire Life Collective on Facebook, for a community of women traveling on the journey of grief to healing. We can't wait to meet you, hear your story, and discover with you where the Lord is leading you on your journey. I personally am so sorry that you have experienced this great loss, and I know that the Lord is seeking to wrap you in His arms. I am honored that he has allowed me to play a small part in His work.

In addition, I suggest you find a trusted individual in your life with whom you can share your thoughts, feelings, and experiences. This could be a friend or family member, counselor, therapist, or an in-person grief group at church or independently. Many times, our thoughts and feelings paralyze us because we are holding them in, and they are literally making us sick and draining us mentally, emotionally, and physically.

You do not have to give a lot of details at first; here are a few suggestions to start making a connection. Go as slow as you need to, one step at a time.

- "I'm struggling right now and just need to talk to someone can we chat?"
- "This is really hard for me to say, but I'm having painful thoughts, and it might help to talk. Are you free?"
- "I don't want to die, but I don't know how to live. Talking with you may help me feel safe. Are you free to talk?"
- "When you get a chance, can you contact me? I feel really alone and suicidal and could use some support."

If you do not have someone in your life and you are having serious thoughts of hurting yourself because the pain is too much to bear, you can also call the suicide hotline at 988. You can talk, text, or chat with a person who is trained to be a listening ear and a shoulder to cry on.

No matter how or who you reach out to, in person or over the phone, don't sit alone in your despair, your pain, your grief and your yearning for things to be different.

Give it to God, allow Him to carry it for you; you were never meant to carry it alone. He paid an immense price with his life to redeem every seemingly small and every completely heartbreaking event of our lives.

He calls you daughter; He is your good Father. When you hurt, He hurts. He suffered so one day you won't have to. In the meantime, He wants to walk every step with you.

JOURNALING

As I have shared, journaling became a lifeline to me very early in my journey. I would feel like if I didn't get something out; then it was going to literally tear me up on the inside and drive my mind crazy. I don't think our bodies and minds are meant to handle the trauma that happens in these situations because we were never designed to do so. It makes sense that it would fight to get it out, to rid itself of the death and destruction that has happened outside of it and is trying to attach to it on the inside. I believe this is why we sometimes fall into a deep depression; our bodies and minds are overwhelmed, and the longer everything is held in, the more damage it causes.

There is freedom in getting our thoughts, feelings, and experiences out, either in writing or verbally. Even if no one ever reads them or hears them, they are now living outside of your mind and body and there is room for the Lord to fill it with promises from him. It also helps you formulate exactly what is happening; oftentimes your mind can feel very jumbled with everything that is happening inside and outside of you. Writing about it will help you navigate those thoughts and feelings and pinpoint if there is a lie you are believing, or a difficult emotion that you are not ready to analyze. Recognizing that it is there is the first step; it will give the Lord the opportunity to bring clarity to it, help you move through it, and analyze it. And often, there will be others who benefit from you navigating that road.

Benefits of journaling through grief:

- Self-awareness - Writing down your thoughts can help you understand how you feel, especially when it's complicated grief.

- Communication - Journaling can help you communicate your feelings with others and be better understood.

- Clarify thoughts - Writing can help you identify patterns of thought and get things out of your head.
- Process emotions - Journaling can help you process intense emotions that come and go unexpectedly.

Tips for journaling through grief:

- Write without worrying about spelling, punctuation, or grammar.
- Don't edit as you write.
- Let yourself lose control and see where it takes you.
- Don't shy away from intense emotions.
- Feel free to get off-topic.
- Reflect on how your grief journey changes over time.

When I think about Adam and Eve in the Garden; after they listened to the devil and questioned God, sin entered the world, and their first inclination was to hide. Then even when God asked them where they were, they had the perfect opportunity to come to God and ask for forgiveness and help navigating feelings of shame. Instead, they started to blame each other, and the death and destruction of that moment started to affect everything inside and around them and all of their relationships in this world. In hiding and keeping their feelings inside, their grief compounded instead of being released and able to dissipate.

Our bodies and minds are not created for carrying grief; that's why when we are constantly watching the events of the news, we start to feel the weight of it physically, mentally, and emotionally. We are finite beings made for life and not death. But we know the infinite One, and we can trust Him with whatever we are thinking, feeling, or experiencing. And maybe one day He will use them to help someone else navigate their journey too, to help them not feel so alone, and to remind them of His faithfulness and love.

This is why I have given you opportunities to journal in this book. Opportunities that you may not have had before, or thought was important. I encourage you to expound as much as possible in your answers to the questions I have listed and add your own as they come up. Mine are just a starting point for the outpouring of all that is inside you. As you lay it all out, your surrender to the Lord will grow, and in your surrender, the Lord can carry you to new heights of faith and trust.

I know I have focused on releasing the hard and difficult thoughts and feelings, but I also invite you to express your gratitude for the small or big blessings you see around you and in you.

Did you get out of bed for the first time today, eat your first meal, take your first shower, have your first real conversation, say a prayer, or feel motivated enough to at least express how you are feeling? These and anything else are victories to be celebrated, moments in which you did not let this tragic, soul-crushing event take you to deep depths of despair. As you celebrate in the hardest of situations, those celebration moments will compound and multiply instead of the grief inside of you. Gratitude for the small will remind your heart and mind of the greatest gift of all, Christ Jesus. Through that lens, your vision and purpose will be renewed and revealed in time.

READING THE BIBLE

I am the type of person who likes to get advice from outside sources, take in information and research topics. If someone mentions they are looking for something, then I am probably going to do research and send them whatever I find. I believe the Lord has blessed me with this gift because here I am, writing a book to be a resource to you and others and using the information I have gathered over the years. This is a blessing and a curse at times because I like to have a lot of information before making a decision; it is difficult for me to trust the Lord fully and blindly.

As Christians, our greatest gift and resource is our Bible, God's word. It is a love letter to us, revealing to us the story of how we have been redeemed by the blood of the lamb through Jesus's sacrifice.

It helps us to know God the Father's character, His design for us to live for His glory and our good. It builds our faith as we read stories of forefathers and mothers in the faith who have gone before us. It's encour-

CHAPTER 11

aging to see the mistakes, valleys, and triumphs of these men and women as it ultimately shines a bright light on God's faithfulness through it all—a faithfulness that is not dependent on our own. It reassures us that we are not walking this road alone, as we walk with the Holy Spirit. John 14:26 says, "But the Helper, the Holy Spirit, whom the Father will send in My name, He will teach you all things and bring to your remembrance all things that I said to you."

The Holy Spirit is also referred to as the Comforter, Counselor, Advocate, and Strengthener. The Bible is the foundation for our life, and as it states, it is the lamp to our feet and a light to our path. (Psalm 119:105)

Considering all those things, it is important for us as Christians to hold it dear and hide its words in our hearts and minds. As I was going to school as a child, we were required to memorize scripture verses, and I now realize what a gift it was to be given that opportunity.

I am reminding us and imploring us to remember the value that we take for granted; there are Christians who must hide to read maybe the few pages of the Bible that they have. There are Christians who have been killed because they believed the teachings of the Bible and distributed it. Let us not take for granted the value we can so easily access in writing or via an audio Bible. Let us instead yearn to spend time in His word and commune with Him.

Reading scriptures during grief can provide significant comfort and support by offering a sense of connection to the God of the universe, reminding us that we are not alone in our pain, providing hope for the future, allowing for the expression of raw emotions, and offering a framework to understand and process loss through biblical stories and teachings about life and death.

Key benefits of reading scriptures during grief:

- Comfort and reassurance: Many scriptures address grief directly, offering words of solace and empathy, reminding you that God is present with you in your pain.

- Hope and perspective: Biblical teachings about eternal life and resurrection can provide a sense of hope beyond earthly loss, helping to reframe grief within a larger perspective.

- Emotional release: The Psalms in particular, offer space to express a wide range of emotions, including anger, sadness, and lament, allowing you to openly grieve without feeling like you need to suppress your feelings.
- Spiritual connection: Engaging with scripture can deepen your connection to God, providing a source of strength and guidance during challenging times.
- Meaning making: By reflecting on biblical stories of loss and redemption, you can find meaning and purpose within your own grief journey.
- Community and support: Sharing scripture with others who are grieving can foster a sense of belonging and shared understanding.

MUSIC + PODCASTS + BOOKS

Music, as we know, is a great way to also learn scripture, as little kids we learned everything put to music. I remember my kids learning the state capitals in a song that they remember every word, even up until now. That is also why it is so important to pay attention to what music we listen to. Especially if it is not Christian music, the words matter as they are getting into your mind, heart and soul.

In 2019, before losing Jonathan, the theology that I believed about God's word and the music I was listening to, were two areas that the Lord was bringing to my attention to examine. He wanted to make sure that my foundation was solid and that I didn't believe that coming to Jesus meant that life would all be good. He wanted to ensure that I knew His character and could decipher the lies of the devil or things that are almost always packaged in partial truths.

I started to drift away from the trendy preachers and listen to more of the sermons that had fewer jokes and personal stories. The sermons that had more of an examination of God's word verse by verse in context. Instead of choosing a topic and finding verses throughout the Bible to fit it, expository preaching allows each verse to teach us something about God and ourselves, in often very difficult situations.

CHAPTER 11

If I had believed on the morning of February 11, 2020, that God wasn't good if bad things happen, that if I had done everything right then this wouldn't have happened, that nothing good would come from this tragic situation—then I would have fallen into a deep pit of anger, blaming God and myself, and depression would have taken over my life.

Instead, I knew and believed with all that I was that God was good no matter what happened in this life. He never wanted us to live in pain or to experience death, but he made a way for it all to be defeated and for us to live in freedom here and in eternity with him. I also knew that although my actions and decisions have consequences in this life, I was not being punished by God. I knew that my God promised that if I received His love, He would work everything together for my good and His glory. I felt the Lord closer and more real that morning as He carried me through the deepest, darkest point of my life.

Music was instrumental in strengthening me, comforting me, building my faith, and empowering me to keep going. It washed over me and helped me to voice my cries to the Lord and praise his name when I had no words of my own. Music helped me to fill my mind with the word of God, to renew my mind, and not let my mind and heart focus on negative thoughts that would pull me into a pit of despair. I would often just sit at the table and have music playing; that way, I was with others and not isolated in my room, and I was sharing the experience of worshipping through music. I have included a playlist of songs in the resources qr code in the back of this book.

Music can be a healthy coping tool for grief. It can help you express your emotions, feel connected to your loved one, and experience a sense of relief. Music can also help you manage your thoughts and adapt to loss.

Podcasts and physical or audiobooks have been a way for me to dive into topics of interest and find mentors who have experienced the same journey or have helped others through it. I would listen to sermons, interviews, and others sharing their own story or the stories of others.

Especially in 2020 when I returned to work and things were very quiet in stores, people did not want a lot of interaction, and we were all wearing masks, so there were visible barriers to connection. I found it a great opportunity to delve into a good podcast or audiobook while I worked; it was my companion as I navigated connecting with others in my new reality. As well as navigating everyone's new reality in the Spring and Summer of 2020.

The interviews and topics were not always about grief, but I did find it comforting to hear how others were walking their journey, how the Lord was carrying them, and the truths that they were holding on to. We are not meant to do this life alone as Christians, and the modern world we live in has made it very accessible to feel connected to others on the same or similar journey.

It's a different way of relating and interacting with others, and it is ok to a certain extent, as long as you don't disconnect completely from those in your real life. We can have a beautiful mixture of the two, just as I am hoping to be for you. We may never meet, but it is my privilege to play a small role in your journey to healing and finding purpose in this season.

COUNSELING

Counseling can be one of the best processes to go through as you journey through grief, and it can be hard to find the right counselor for you. It's ok to audition grief counselors to find the right fit. Within that, you will need to consider if you want individual, couples, or family counseling depending on your need or situation. I have seen a few different counselors/therapists over the years, and they were all unique with different strengths. I saw them for different reasons as well.

My first was after having my 2nd daughter, Katie, in 2007. My pregnancy with her was very stressful, and I didn't get much rest physically or mentally. I had been given a lot of responsibilities at work, we moved houses shortly after she was born, and I was finishing my bachelor's degree online. My body and mind were completely depleted, and I was also trying to sustain a newborn, the rest of the family, and work after my maternity leave was over.

My sister took me into the psychiatric hospital when she didn't know what else to do; I had no energy or excitement for anything. Mind you, I have never been an overly exuberant person, as I am naturally an introvert. So, I imagine I must have been in a desperate state.

CHAPTER 11

I wasn't threatening to hurt myself or others, so they thought I could improve without hospitalization or medication. They gave me a referral for a therapist and honestly if my mood was improving, then she diagnosed me as doing better. She was not the type of therapist to dig into your past trauma and wounds and get to the root of anything. She was purely to address the current state and how I could get to a better place daily.

A few years after that, Anthony and I went to couples' therapy. She was "Christian" based but very light on that front. It was his idea that we go; it did help in some ways. To be able to see that we wanted to work toward the same things, but we had very different viewpoints on how to get there or what was causing us not to. Our relationship was great while we were going. The sessions gave us an opportunity to spend time with each other each week, as we would usually go to the appointment and then go on a date night after. It helped us appreciate each other, feel united, and work toward goals together.

In my opinion, neither dug into where the trauma came from that created the beliefs we individually had, what core desires we were trying to fulfill or run from in our childhood, etc., and without us both doing work to discover and uproot those things; most other work was just surface level. I have learned that unless you heal your wounds, they will just keep coming up in different ways.

With only surface level work, then it is easy to revert to old patterns and habits and that is what happened to us. Shortly after we stopped going to our weekly sessions and date nights were put on the back burner, then our distance and misunderstandings returned.

My last individual counselor experience thus far was right after Jonathan passed away. Friends insisted I go see someone as I seemed to be handling things too well, even though I was verbally expressing and sharing my ups and downs. So, I went and the person they gave me was younger, and as I was sharing my feelings, she was the one crying. I could see that my experience was greatly impacting her, and I felt like I was the one comforting her. I did not continue with her. Shortly after that, we started family grief counseling, and in my opinion, this was one of the best things we could do as a family at that time.

We were all receiving the information and advice and were given the opportunity together to verbally process with an outside source. We did not have to help our girls navigate this situation alone while trying to navigate it ourselves. Kids often take things better from an outside source, even if you would tell them the same thing. I think it helped the girls to understand why we were each coping in different ways and gave them information on why and how to grieve individually and together. She explained the stages of grief, different ways to celebrate special occasions, and how to view what had happened, the present, and the future.

One of the best pieces of advice I remember that she gave us was to view Jonathan as someone who lived nine full years of life, not someone who died at 9 years old. That may seem simple, but it shifted my mind around how I viewed losing him, the time we had with him, and our future without him.

Above everything I think it gave the girls an opportunity to process everything that maybe we as adults were processing on our own; but as children they really didn't know what and how to process.

Our family counselor was faith based, she seemed to have a Christian perspective but also a respect for other faiths, she didn't use scripture a lot but did reference God and his goodness etc. Anthony was not a Christian, so I think the Christian light approach was better for him to receive from.

My most recent therapy and counseling group experience came into my life just last year. It was a 4-month program that included one weekend a month of 10 hours of immersive interaction with the coaches and other students. We unveiled trauma from our childhood and throughout our lives and really dug into what lies we had believed and wounds we had because of these situations and occurrences. How we were living our lives based on these lies, how we and others were missing out or paying the price due to these wounds, and what our true identity was in Christ. It truly uprooted my lies of unworthiness; thinking I was not likable because I wasn't an extrovert. Also, how I suppressed my emotions and not connected to them, so I was not able to connect with others emotionally, relationally, sexually, and more.

This was most effective because I wasn't only just treating how I was manifesting these wounds in my life. I was going deep and uprooting them and analyzing how they had played out and were playing out in each area of life. This was the first time that I was truly emotionally mature or intelligent and was now able to assess what was happening inside my head and heart at the moment and combat it with the truth of God's word and the truth of the situation.

All of these experiences taught me different things as I observed the different therapists, my reaction to their methods and how I left that experience. I was able to hone into what was effective and what wasn't. Looking back I can see even more all that the Lord was teaching me and how He is using all of it to help you navigate this season.

You may not know what prerequisites to have if this is your first time looking for a therapist/counselor. Or maybe you have had less than a desirable experience in the past, so here are a few suggestions to keep in mind to find a Christian counselor.

Ask for recommendations from your church community, pastors, or trusted friends and family members who have used Christian counseling services. Search online directories through professional organizations like the American Association of Christian Counselors. Reach out to Christian organizations like Focus on the Family; and consider asking your regular healthcare provider for a referral to a Christian counselor.

Counselors: Focus on providing short-term, solution-oriented support for specific issues such as relationship problems, career guidance, or life transitions.

Therapists: May address a wider range of mental health concerns, including diagnosed disorders, and provide more in-depth and long-term therapy.

Key points to consider when searching for a Christian counselor or therapist:

- Check credentials: Ensure the counselor is licensed and has appropriate training in Christian counseling.

- Ask about their approach: Inquire about their specific Christian perspective on counseling and how they integrate faith into therapy.

- Consider your needs: Think about what specific issues you want to address and whether the counselor specializes in those areas.

- Interview potential counselors: Schedule a consultation call or in-person meeting to discuss your needs and get a sense of their style and compatibility.

There is one organization that I want to point out to you— Nothing Is Wasted Ministries. I have not experienced their trauma/grief counseling, but I have listened to their podcast and have read the founder's book; both have helped me greatly. They specialize in walking through the grief journey with you individually or in groups with counselors trained in trauma/grief therapy. From what I have seen from them, they will be helpful in navigating the current trauma that has resulted from losing your child, addressing past hurts, and analyzing how the two are interwoven into the present. They will offer to help you discover a path for the future. I will include them in the resources qr code at the end of this book.

You can also find grief groups at many churches, yours may even have one. It is often helpful to be around others experiencing the same thing and may be more effective than individual counseling because you will gain community as well and prevent self-isolation. Often there is a curriculum that is followed and weekly meetings.

Above all, no matter the avenue you choose to pursue to help you sort out, investigate, or navigate your journey of grief, I have realized that only the Holy Spirit can do lasting work. He can use others to help you, but He does the heart and soul work. So, whether you do or don't pursue outside help, know that He is walking through every season and every step with you. Ask him to comfort you and give you joy, to search your heart, to strengthen you, to reveal the truth to you about Him and yourself, and to give you clarity and purpose for the road ahead.

RELEASE + CREATE ENERGY

Each step we've talked about so far has mostly included your mind and heart, feelings, emotions, thoughts and releasing a wide range— so you don't explode. There are also things we can do that don't require us to talk, reflect, dig deep, express gratitude or write everything out. What if I

CHAPTER 11

told you there were helpful things you can do that don't require you to think deeply at all? Yes, please!

Here are some suggestions that you can add your own to: exercise, cooking, watching movies, playing games, and dancing. What else would you add to this list?

Let's first talk about exercise, you could play basketball, football, pickleball, soccer, tennis, ride bikes, run, walk, swim or lift weights. Do anything that is going to release energy from your body and produce energy in your body. Personally, I have never been a big competitive sport type of person, such as basketball or football, so my go-to early on was walking and bike riding.

Benefits of exercise:

- Releases endorphins, which can help relieve pain and stress and improve your mood
- Help you sleep better
- Exercise can help reduce levels of cortisol, a stress hormone that can be elevated during grief
- Boost your energy levels
- Give you a sense of accomplishment
- Improve your self-esteem
- Helps you connect with others who are going through similar experiences

How to exercise while grieving:

- Exercising outdoors can help you feel more at peace
- Combine exercise with other forms of emotional support: Talk to friends, family, or a therapist
- Be patient with yourself: Give yourself time to heal and trust that you will feel better again

Next let's explore cooking and baking and how they can also be beneficial in that they can offer comfort and normalcy during grief. Providing a temporary escape and a way to feel connected to loved ones despite your loss. You may feel close to your loved one by making their favorite dish or dessert or expanding your culinary skills, if that was something they enjoyed.

Cooking is a sensory experience involving touch, taste, sight, smell, and hearing. Of all the senses, the sense most strongly tied to memory is olfactory, aka our sense of smell. When we cook, we activate the hippocampus and amygdala, which are parts of the brain involved in memory and emotional processing.

Cooking helps us grieve by minimizing the fear of forgetting our loved ones, whether it's their voice, their laugh, or that one facial expression they had when they were about to sneeze. Knowing that our sense of smell is powerfully tied to memories means that we can access them when cooking dishes we associate with our loved ones. By following recipes that our loved ones used to make for us or recreating dishes we once shared, we keep the memory of a loved one or past experience alive.

For me it is less about the actual cooking and more about remembering things like how Jonathan would stir his ice cream until it was all soft and melted instead of eating it frozen solid. How he really didn't like Chicken Kitchen bowls, and how when he made a Nutella sandwich, he would lick his fingers at least 10 times.

Similar to exercise, dance is very therapeutic. Do you like to dance? At the beginning of 2023, I stepped way out of my comfort zone and normal activities and took a ballroom dancing class. I had a great time, and it built my confidence and allowed me to explore a different part of myself. I would love to get back to it one day as I had to stop due to schedule and cost. I would recommend everyone try to take at least one class. It's like learning a new language in vocabulary and body language. Of course, there is also the option of more natural and spontaneous dancing in your bedroom, at family parties, or weddings, etc.

Dance has been in many cultures, a way of communicating without words and has brought peace and started wars, so don't discount the ability to tell your story through dance. Even if you are just dancing to express/tell your story for yourself or to God. In the Bible, David used dance to express himself during many different seasons of life. He danced out of excitement and joy to acknowledge God's presence and blessings, to seek God's pardon and mercy, and to surrender to God in worship.

Dancing can be a therapeutic way to process grief because it can help you express emotions, connect with others, and feel peace.

Emotional release:

- Dancing can help you release pent-up emotions and feel relief.
- It can help you explore your grief and heal invisible wounds.
- It can help you move through difficult parts of your story.

Connection with others:

- Dancing in a group can help you feel less alone and build camaraderie.
- The sense of community can help you feel supported and connected.

Physical health:

- Dance therapy can improve motor coordination and other physical health.
- Movement can change your internal chemical state and help you feel better.
- Dancing can help release tension in your body.

Self expression:

- Dance can be a way to express yourself without using words.
- You can use your body movement to tell a story and convey your feelings.

Mental health:

- Dance can help manage anxiety, depression, and other mental health challenges.

- It can help you process feelings of loss.

WATCHING MOVIES + PLAYING GAMES

For me, the movies I choose to watch depend on my mood because there are movies that bring back memories of watching them with Jonathan; or maybe he watched them over and over, like Madagascar and The Lego Movie. So, I must decide if I want to take myself back to those times or not. Usually, I choose yes, but I know that I have the opportunity, to choose no. Movies also help you escape the moment and memories sometimes. A funny movie or a movie with characters or a plot so different from your life can be relaxing.

There was one movie that I watched after Jonathan passed away, Frozen 2. I wasn't warned of how much the events would closely resemble our family, as the characters were already special to us. My girls were always Elsa and Anna, and Jonathan, of course, was Olaf, so if you know the story, Olaf passes away (but does come back). It gave me a moment of pause but then a sweet moment to cherish Jonathan and be thankful for him.

When we played games, Jonathan was in the same room, often dancing to music, creating a game of his own, or helping someone play their turn. He liked playing checkers or tic tac toe and games like that, but for older, more complicated games, he would sit them out. I remember one of the first times we played a game as just us 4. There was a picture of Jonathan close by, and it was as if he was still there, just watching us. I smiled at it and took a picture with my phone and thought to myself how there can be so many emotions all wrapped up in one and happening at the same time. There was the joy and enjoyment of the 4 of us having fun together but also missing a member of the family.

Watching movies and playing games while grieving can act as a form of distraction and emotional escape, providing temporary relief from the

CHAPTER 11

overwhelming feelings of loss, allowing you to process your grief at your own pace within a controlled environment. Sometimes even offering opportunities to connect with themes of loss and healing presented in the narrative of the media they choose; essentially acting as a coping mechanism to manage the difficult emotions associated with grief.

Key points about using movies and games as a coping mechanism for grief:

- Distraction: Immersing oneself in a fictional world can temporarily take the mind off the painful reality of loss, providing a much-needed break from emotional distress.

- Emotional processing: Certain movies and games explore themes of loss, death, and grief, allowing you to indirectly engage with your own emotions by relating to characters experiencing similar situations.

- Sense of control: When playing games, you can actively participate in the narrative, providing a sense of agency and control over your experience, which can be comforting during a time of feeling powerless.

- Social connection: Online multiplayer games can provide a space for connecting with others, sharing experiences, and finding support from a community.

CHAPTER 12

FAMILY

MARRIAGE AFTER LOSS

I have shared glimpses from my perspective of the troubles in my marriage throughout this book, and I know that us losing Jonathan did not help our already unstable foundation. I also know that losing him was not the cause of our divorce. I can only speak about my own experience, and I want to be respectful of Anthony's privacy, so will not speculate on his reason for leaving or share too many details. However, I know that whether circumstantial due to work schedules or my doing or Anthony's; over the years it was usually just the kids and me that would spend the most time together. Then, when it became just us girls and Anthony, it created a wider divide without that other male energy from Jonathan. In my opinion, we, for the most part, were a family but not really also a couple. It is very important for the health of your marriage for there to be a distinct and separate relationship and focus on the husband and wife outside of their roles as parents in the family unit.

Initially, after losing Jonathan, we were major supporters of each other; we had intimate times of comforting each other, as I have shared. Neither of us felt resentful or shut out by the other's grieving process. I think that the family counseling greatly helped with this as it naturally welcomed each other into how we were processing or coping, without feeling awkward in having to ask.

We did not fall into a deep hole of despair that we felt helpless to pull the other out of, and we didn't experience a breaking of our marriage in this season. But we did return to being more disconnected, as had happened many times before. Possibly because that romantic, in-love, connected soul, favorite person in the world relationship had never really been our story.

We were connected through our experience and had a new appreciation for each other as we had just survived the worst loss imaginable. Maybe it also made Anthony realize even more that life was short, and he wanted to try to have that connection with someone else.

Of course, I will always believe that we were also missing the foundation and connection of both of us first living to serve and love Christ and then each other. That was missing all throughout our marriage and continued after Jonathan passed away. But as a common grace from the Lord, there are many marriages where neither of the spouses is Christian, and they have a very happy, healthy, committed, fulfilling marriage. Just as there are many Christian marriages that choose not to honor their commitments. I do believe that the combination of the two is best; Jesus is Lord of both and there is a natural attraction and affection for each other. I also believe that with Jesus as Lord, there are times that the attraction and affection can grow on a much deeper level, if maybe it wasn't there before.

For me, I think if we had gotten divorced before losing Jonathan, we would have a different view and place in our hearts for each other.

We will always be the mother and father of each other's children, but losing Jonathan and walking through that grieving journey together took that connection to a deeper level, that most will never experience or understand. And I would never wish this connection on anyone, either.

Statistics say that 90% of married couples experience relationship problems following the death of their child; the divorce rate is about 30%. Which is actually lower than the average divorce rate for couples who don't experience child loss.

The death of a child can cause significant emotional turmoil for a couple. However, many marriages survive this difficult time. Staying married after the death of your child is possible with courage, vulnerability, and love. It also takes a lot of grace, patience, and understanding that your spouse will change in small and big ways through this journey, and so will you. As you discover new ways about you, share with your spouse and be eager to discover their new ways as well. Grow together on the journey through the different seasons of life.

It is comforting for me to know that most marriages do, in fact, survive the loss of a child. So, if you find yourself and your husband struggling, here are some words of advice.

With Jesus as your foundation, seek Him in all that you do and say, pray for him to fortify your marriage, to guard it against anything that would try to pull you apart. Deepen your love and relationship with Him, and allow that love, grace, mercy, and joy to overflow out of you onto your spouse and everyone around you.

This, in addition to practical work on both sides, is vital to every marriage during seasons of heartbreaking grief or seasons of joy and celebration.

Navigating grief while strengthening your marriage:

- Communicate: Share feelings of hopelessness, confusion, anger, depression, or guilt.

- Seek therapy: A therapist can help couples work through their grief and rebuild their relationship.

- Be patient: Grief can take months or years.

- Avoid major decisions: Try not to make big decisions like moving or changing careers in the first year after the loss.

- Focus on each other: Plan activities your spouse enjoys or prepare their favorite meal.

- Allow each other space: Accept disappointment and provide space for each other's grief.

Challenges to be aware of:

- Changes in identity: The death of a child can change you and your family forever.

- Decreased intimacy: The death of a child can lead to decreased sexual intimacy.

- Difficulty communicating: The death of a child can make it harder to communicate emotionally.

SIBLINGS

As you know from reading my story, Jonathan has 2 sisters, Alayna and Katelyn. He was the youngest, the baby of the family and his two older sisters had a special relationship with him in very different ways. This of course happens in all families because of ages, interests, gender and other factors. Just as their relationship was different, so was their need for how they journeyed through grief.

    Alayna was the oldest sister who had started to spend more time with friends instead of her siblings, so she experienced some guilt for not being around Buddy as much as she thought she maybe should have been. We reassured her that she did not need to feel guilty about it, that life develops and changes and that it is normal. She was a great help to her brother; Buddy knew that she loved him so much and he loved her too. Alayna was also the first one to discover Jonathan not breathing that morning. I imagine there was a lot of shock to her very unsuspecting body, heart, and mind.

    Considering everything, Alayna returned to her swim practice very quickly the next day. I think she wanted to do something that felt normal and routine. It was probably a great way for her to get the energy out that she was feeling. She could push herself to fight through the water. It helped her to be around people who loved her and be active, but she also experienced anxiety attacks when she was under the water for a while. Her coach contacted us a few times and let us know that she would come

CHAPTER 12

up crying and have difficulty breathing. He would have her sit out for a bit; I imagine the flashbacks were very difficult, as they were for all of us.

Both girls returned to school on February 13th, 2 days after losing their brother. Katie stayed with her best friend, Gabi, the night before and rode to school with her that morning. I texted her teacher to let her know that she was returning to school. We both thought it was too soon, but Katie came to me and told me that she wanted to go back to school. Several of her friends had come and visited us the two previous days and her entire class had taken the news very hard when they heard. Her teacher told me that she would be there for her and the entire class. She would also notify the school counselor in case she needed to come back in to meet with all of them again, with Katie present.

I told her teacher that since I wasn't dropping her off and Buddy would usually be in the car, then maybe the drop-off situation and process being completely different, would be a little easier. A totally new experience, instead of a haunting absence of J's presence in the car. That day would come, but there at least wouldn't be so many new things being faced at the same time.

I just looked back at my text communication with Katie during that time, I had forgotten all the time that she spent at her best friend's house that first week. I couldn't remember where she slept, but I see now that she was sleeping outside of our house and not in her room or bed. I wonder if she felt abandoned by me, like I had all these things to manage for her brother in a different way than ever before, and I wasn't able to be there for her in all the ways I usually would. I think she also needed her own escape.

I thanked Gabi's mom, Cari, as her house provided a place of stability for Katie during that time. She said that it was her pleasure as she wanted to be for Katie, who she needed when she lost her brother several years ago. She could relate to what Katie was going through.

Alayna must have been dropped off by her dad on her first day back at school. I texted her to call me if she needed to and then I checked on her a few hours later. She said she was ok for the most part and cried a little when her teacher and assistant principal pulled her to the side to talk to her.

There is a special video that she watched over and over that day to help her make it through. It is a video of Jonathan talking about how many pancakes he wants and how he wants to put them on Alayna's head instead of eating them.

This video is part of a shared photo album that I know we all revisit on occasion and we will reference a photo or video to bring each other into that memory.

We were very lucky to have support and care from all areas of our life – schools, church, swim club, family and friends. We were the type of family where if you knew one child then you knew their siblings as well. We were always at each other's performances, races, school events and friend's birthday parties. If mom got to be there, the others were probably going to be there too. I wouldn't have wanted it any other way.

The next week, leading up to Jonathan's celebration, life slowly took on a new routine of friends and family helping to transport the girls and offer them some sense of normalcy. While their dad and I tried to tackle this journey that we were suddenly thrust into. I can see how during that time, they may have felt pushed to the side most of the time as they were watching me and their dad trying to maneuver our own grief.

We started family counseling on March 7th. Less than a full month after Jonathan passed away. In some ways, we had all been carrying this burden individually and dealing with school, practice, planning, parenting, making decisions, battling the flashbacks, and everything else in our own way. As we entered those sessions, we were all learning together, growing and evolving as a family of 4.

In conversation with Alayna in the present, she told me that she felt cared for and supported; she didn't see how events of that morning would have been better navigated if done differently. Some situations you just survive, this was one of them.

To comfort other siblings after the death of a child, acknowledge their feelings, allow them to express their grief openly, share memories of the loved one, reassure them that their feelings are valid.

Offer practical support while respecting their need for space and time to process the loss; importantly, let them know it's okay to feel sad, angry, or confused, and that they are not alone in their grief.

Key points to remember:

- Validate their emotions: Say things like, "It's okay to feel sad," or "It's normal to miss your sibling."
- Share memories: Bring up positive stories about your loved one to help keep their memory alive.
- Ask open-ended questions: Encourage them to talk about their feelings without pressuring them to elaborate if they don't want to.
- Be present and listen actively: Simply being there to listen without judgment can be incredibly comforting.
- Offer practical help: Ask if they need help with errands, schoolwork, or other daily tasks.
- Reassure them it's not their fault: Address any potential guilt they might feel by reminding them that the death was not their responsibility.
- Model healthy coping mechanisms: Share your own emotions appropriately to show them it's okay to grieve.
- Respect their boundaries: Understand that they may need time alone or to express their grief in their own way.

What to avoid:

- Minimizing their feelings: Don't say things like "They're in a better place now" or "You'll get over this."
- Pressuring them to talk: If they don't want to discuss the loss, respect their wishes.
- Making comparisons: Avoid comparing their grief to others' experiences.
- Giving unsolicited advice: Unless asked, don't offer quick solutions or try to fix their grief.

- If you are concerned about a sibling's grief, consider seeking professional help from a therapist specializing in child bereavement.

CELEBRATIONS

Today, February 11, 2025, as I'm writing this part of my book, it is the 5th anniversary of Jonathan passing away. Today was the first time in the last 5 years that my 17-year-old daughter, Katie, asked me specifically if we could go to the cemetery. I share this with you to encourage you to always leave the door open for communication about what they need or want. It has been years since I asked how they would like to celebrate milestones and holidays. Understand that we are all just trying to figure out what life looks like now and what we need or want to change by day sometimes.

I know that many times, as the mom in our family, I set the stage for certain holidays in the first year. I think this came with the territory of leading the way before our loss and everyone looking to me to lead us. For instance, on our first Christmas in 2020, I wanted the 4 of us to be together. This was different than we usually would do in other years; many times, the three kids would go to Ohio with my sister, and some years, I would go as well. I couldn't imagine going there without Jonathan and continuing as usual, so I needed to do something that was completely not what we would usually do.

I received a lot of grace from my family, especially in this, because I know that the excitement and magic of the holidays that my sister creates is something my girls look forward to every year.

Our Christmas day was much quieter and more what I needed, but possibly not what the rest of the family needed, but out of love, they were there for me.

It's ok to try celebrating in one way and then decide that it didn't produce what you were wanting or just that it doesn't need to be like that again the next year. Give everyone grace in the process.

I knew on the 2nd anniversary of Jonathan's passing that would probably be the last time we would all gather in the cemetery as a family

CHAPTER 12

of 4. Anthony had moved out, and then Alayna would be away at college next year. Our family was changing even more over time, and I had to be okay with that and hold everything loosely. Thankfully, the biggest blow had happened first, and each subsequent disappointment or change seemed a little less traumatic or difficult than the last. I see this as a grace from the Lord for our family, a grace for peace, closure, and transition.

When grieving the loss of a loved one, you can celebrate birthdays, holidays, and anniversaries in ways that honor the person and your feelings.

Ideas for commemorating:

- Create a tradition: Light a candle, make a cake, or visit a favorite place
- Share memories: Invite friends to share photos and stories
- Honor the person: Donate to a charity, plant a tree, or create a memorial
- Celebrate their life: Attend a concert or game they enjoyed
- Get support: Ask friends for help or join a support group
- Allow yourself to feel: Don't feel guilty about laughing or having fun

YOUR CHILD'S OLD ROOM + BELONGINGS

Anthony and I would agree that we cleaned out Jonathan's things too quickly; it hadn't even been a month when my mom and I went through and donated most of his things. I think I decided to do it for a few reasons: we were all sitting around, and I wanted to feel "productive." And also, I wanted to give Katie her own space and thought maybe those things were haunting her; at the time, some of them seemed to be just random things that didn't hold any sentiment, worth, or energy.

We were very wrong; as we sorted through, we selected things to keep as very special items that depicted certain times or something that Jonathan loved, such as little bouncy balls, his Star Wars piggy bank, his science devotional book, his lightsaber, his Nerf guns and bullets, and his walkie-talkies among other things. We scooped everything else into a garbage bag, and Anthony took it to the donation site. We felt the weight of removing those things from the house almost instantly; the little boy, Jonathan energy, left with them. We were so impacted that Anthony drove back to the donation site and asked to look through the bags again and pulled out a few more things to keep.

If I could do it all again, then I would wait longer to clean out his things, maybe go through a couple of times just organizing and grouping things and taking it slowly in deciding what will stay and what will go. Once I took them out of the actual room, I would place them in the garage or another room for a time before removing them from the house completely.

The way we did it was like we just ripped the band-aid off, and the wound was still bleeding and needed protection and care. We recovered, but I still wish we had done it differently.

We know that our things become part of our personality and take on our energy and who we are, and I think we can get focused on what others may think and what we should be doing at this point or if something is taking too long. Early on especially, give yourself grace and it is better to wait a little too long than remove things too early and regret it. To display some little special things that I did keep, I ordered small mason jars from Amazon and created keepsakes featuring items that made Buddy, Buddy.

His Spiderman watch, his Stormtrooper wallet, his little bendable man, his little red flashlight. I have 3 for myself in the living room, and Anthony, Alayna, and Katie all have one that they keep wherever they choose. I also have his basket of Legos, laser tag game, and cars available for any little kids to play with when they visit.

Sorting through a loved one's belongings while grieving can be an emotionally challenging process, so it's important to be patient with yourself, seek support from others, and take breaks when needed; categorize items into "keep," "donate," and "discard" piles, and consider creating a memorial with a few meaningful keepsakes to honor their memory.

CHAPTER 12

Key points to remember:

- Gather support: Don't try to do this alone; ask family members or close friends to help you sort through items, especially if you're feeling overwhelmed.
- Communicate with family: Discuss with other family members who might have an interest in certain items, ensuring a fair distribution of heirlooms.
- Be kind to yourself: Take your time, don't rush, and stop when you need to; acknowledge your emotions and allow yourself to grieve.
- Categorize items: Label boxes or areas as "keep," "donate," "give to family," and "discard" to help with organization.
- Create a memorial: Choose a few special items to display as a tangible reminder of your loved one, such as photos, favorite jewelry, or clothing.
- Consider professional help: If needed, reach out to a grief counselor or professional organizer for guidance.

GRACE FOR YOURSELF + OTHERS

There are many things that we all say in times of mourning, and we may even say them to ourselves, but they are not helpful, comforting, nice, or true. Even as someone who has gone through many different forms of loss and grief, I even find myself thinking and saying the "inappropriate" thing at times.

Most people don't intend to bring guilt, shame, confusion, or insensitive platitudes at that moment, but I think each of our bodies, minds, and hearts go into a sense of shock and coping, and the comments that come out may reflect that. An immense amount of grace and compassion is needed when you find yourself on either end, whether that's making a comment or the one receiving it, as most of us are not equipped to process everything at that moment. Many times, friends and family are at a loss for words and truly do not know what to say, so to avoid what they perceive as awkward silence, they say something that ends up hurting or invalidating your feelings or experience.

Grace is also needed if we possibly react at that moment in a way that we later think was inappropriate as well. It is understandable that you, too, are trying to make sense of everything bombarding your heart and mind. I think that saying, "Hurt people, hurt people," can be effective here. We are all hurting, and that hurt, and maybe layers of hurt from our own experiences and beliefs often culminates in our interactions throughout our lives in different ways. The loss of a child, being one of the most sensitive, heartbreaking moments, surely does not exempt us from these interactions.

Some things that may be said:

- Don't feel bad. At least you have other children
- Be grateful for the time you had together
- Grief just takes time
- She wouldn't want you to be sad
- Stay strong for your wife/husband/kids
- You must move forward and go on with your life
- Everything happens for a reason
- You can always have other children
- Just give it time
- You never get over the loss of a child
- Grief is your new normal
- God needed another angel in Heaven
- At least he's no longer suffering
- Throw yourself into your work

CHAPTER 12

- He's at peace now
- I know exactly how you feel
- She went to be with God
- Remodel their bedroom as soon as you can so you're not reminded of them
- Don't throw away any of his stuff, or you'll regret it

We can see how these comments can elicit some gut reactions and bring back emotions from when we heard them, thought them, or said them. Are some of them true? Of course. Are they needed at that moment? Possibly or probably not. Are a lot of them based on opinions that contradict each other? Yes, and many times, our opinions, unless specifically asked for, are not needed in those situations. I would say that many are much more complicated and layered than just a blanket statement. Let me address a couple specifically.

"You never get over the loss of your child" and "Grief is your new normal." These two things are true to an extent, and I would like to share my experience with them.

The loss and longing that you have for your child no longer being in your life, not experiencing them grow up and discovering their interests or career or any of the milestones of this beautiful life, surely you do not get over it. That will never go away because you will and should long for that time and that physical, tangible love you once shared. It is because of that love that this loss and longing will forever remain. The hope that I would like to give to you, from my experience and the experience of many others, is that—the heart-breaking, soul-crushing, debilitating pain of the loss of your child, however, will not always remain.

This reality is because the second statement of grief is your new normal; it surely will become a part of every fiber of your being. It will forever change you, how you view others around you, and life in general. In the early stages, it will be all you think about, all you think others think about you, and often all that you want to talk about, and others want to talk about with you. This is a normal reaction, and this is how we process any major change in our lives. I am here to be a witness to the fact that losing your child is a change that is not normal, and it is ok for our body, mind, and heart to often take an immense amount of time to adjust to this new normal.

Through this adjustment process, through lamenting with the Lord in each stage and through the gift of life continuing to evolve and change, your life will grow around your grief. Where once it consumed your thoughts and energy, you will slowly find that you are able to think about and focus on other things. You will integrate your new life together with your journey through grief.

Let me also get in front of the guilt you may feel from these new developments; you may start to feel as though you are betraying your child. You may think that if your immense grief of losing them starts to be less all-encompassing, then so is your love for them. This could not be farther from the truth. If anything, that love for them has become even more of who you are; having been given the chance to love them has shaped you forever. How you have changed, grown, and evolved as you now learn how to navigate life without them by your side, is a testament to the impact that love has had on you.

I believe that as you journey through grief, it is something that feels like it's waiting to attack you from the outside at any moment. It's a foreign experience and feeling, and as you realize that the amount of grief you are feeling is conversely related to the amount of love you share with them, then you are able to pull it close, and it becomes more sacred instead of scary.

For the next time we are at a loss for words, here are a few reminders or suggestions. I will be honest; I am not the best at most of these so I will be revisiting this list often.

- Listen Actively: Offer a compassionate ear without interrupting or offering unsolicited advice. Let them talk about their loved ones and memories. Let them express anger or frustration without judging them. Allow them to express their emotions freely.

- Be Present: Sometimes, your physical presence is more comforting than words. Offer to prepare or bring a meal. Offer to do laundry, clean the house, or any other household chores. Offer to pick up groceries, prescriptions, or other necessities. Assist with sorting out paperwork/other kinds of belongings. Offer to walk their dog or care for their pets.

If they have children, offer to watch them for a few hours. Assist in managing their bills if they're struggling. If they have hobbies, join them in their favorite activities. If they're feeling too emotional, offer to drive them where they need to go. If possible, offer to help manage their work responsibilities.

- Acknowledge Their Loss: Simple phrases like "I'm so sorry for your loss" can be significant. Sometimes, a hug can convey more than words. Avoid phrases like "They're in a better place."

- Send a Card, Flowers, or Gift: A handwritten note can show that you care. A small, meaningful gift can provide comfort. Flowers can be a comforting reminder that you're thinking of them. A care package can include comfort food, teas, candles, and a comforting book about grief and healing.

- Check-In Regularly: Continue to check in weeks and months after the loss. Continue to reach out even after the initial shock has worn off. Remind them to care for themselves, whether just a walk or a nap. Send them reminders to eat, drink water, and rest. Suggest they write down their feelings.

- Share Memories: If you know the deceased, share positive memories with your friend or family member.

- Be Patient: Grieving takes time; let them grieve at their own pace. Validate their emotions, whatever they may be.

- Respect Their Space: Sometimes they might need time alone; respect their need for space. Pay attention to what they say they need and try to provide it. Understand that everyone copes differently. Don't push for details they aren't ready to share.

- Attend the Funeral: If you're close enough, attend the funeral or memorial service.

- Help Plan a Tribute: Assist in planning a tribute or memorial for their loved one. Help them compile photos and stories into a memory book. Do something symbolic in memory of their loved one. Donate to a charity in the deceased's name.

- Plan a Day Out: Help them take their mind off things by planning a simple outing. Sometimes, a distraction, like a movie or a game, can help. Gentle exercise can be a great way to provide support.

- Celebrate Anniversaries and Plan for Holidays: Remember the dates that are important to them and offer support during these times. Holidays can be challenging; offer to spend them together or help them plan.

- Encourage Professional Help: Suggest they talk to a therapist if they're open to it. Help them find or start a support group.

- Share the Gospel: Give them hope for beyond this life and for new life now. The ability to lay all their worries and burdens at the feet of Jesus. They can put their trust in Him.

CHAPTER 13

LOGISTICS

MOVING

At the end of February 2022, the girls and I moved out of our house; you may remember the journal entry where I talked about it. Anthony had already moved out. Our landlords lived out of state and no longer wanted to keep the house and maintain it from so far away. They offered for us to purchase it at a price lower than they would sell it otherwise, but during that time, housing prices were so inflated that it was out of reach completely.

This move meant that we would be leaving the home that held all of our last memories of Jonathan. It was sad for us to leave the house; that house and neighborhood had been a very sweet season for our family much of the time. When we moved into it, we were leaving some difficult years of struggling financially and all three kids living in one room in our small two-bedroom townhouse.

At that time, our finances had become more stable, and we were on a good stint as we were in marriage counseling, and that always brought some reprieve from the disconnection and strife that often existed between Anthony and me. This house was very special to our kids, and I know that as they look back on their childhood, this will be the house they remember. Even more than the house itself, the neighborhood and, specifically, The Neighbors were the best part and hardest part to leave behind.

When the times weren't so good again with Anthony and me, The Neighbors were a place of love, lightheartedness, and laughter. They were extra siblings and an additional Tia, Tio, Abuela, and Abuelo to my kids. Beatriz and I have spent countless hours texting, talking in person, and on the phone about mom stuff, marriage, things we agree and disagree about, the questions of life and death, planning for the future, and reminiscing about the past. The Lord really blessed us richly and quickly knitted our hearts together. Whether living across the street or across the world, we are forever in each other's corner.

Cleaning everything out of the house was very difficult; we were now having to go through everything like we had with Jonathan's things because we were downsizing and had accumulated quite a bit in the 5 years living there. It's like they say, "If there is a space, you will fill it." We were also going through another type of grieving process as we sorted through items from almost 18 years of marriage and all the years of our kids' lives.

This would be the first time that we would not be moving as a family and the first time we would also not be moving with Jonathan. So many emotions and so much compounded grief for everyone involved.

The grief of losing a member of our family and then losing the family altogether as we knew it and then losing the house where we were a family with all its members intact. As well as all the things you must tackle now as a single mom making all the decisions alone and many for the first time.

Give yourself grace, constantly lay everything at the feet of Jesus, ask for help, allow yourself to cry, and feel the weight of the moment or season. Know that mistakes may be made, and that's okay; things may not be exactly how you want them or expected they would be, so keep your eyes on The One who holds the future in His hands. Hold fast to the promise that He will never leave you or forsake you, whether in this house, apartment, city, or country. In this season or the next, He will be your constant, your foundation, and your ultimate HOME.

CHAPTER 13

This was my/our experience of having to move, and we actually moved again a year later and had to downsize even more. Maybe your situation is different, and you actually feel like you need to leave a traumatic experience. Maybe the memories of your child not being there anymore are hard for you, and a fresh start would invite you to cherish those memories but give you some space from them as well. Or you may end up feeling too far away from those memories, kind of like when I donated Jonathan's things. All those things held his energy, and so did our home.

The most important thing is to recognize what you are feeling and why; don't try to mask your feelings and pretend they are not there. Also realize that just a change of location won't remove those feelings completely, as those feelings are most likely much deeper than a specific place. Be as realistic as you can in that season, which I know can be difficult as you are trying to navigate uncharted waters and often just keep the boat from being taken over by the waves of grief, to keep from going under.

Be mindful that moving can be stressful and might not be the right choice for everyone in the midst of grief; consult with loved ones and a therapist and weigh the practical reasons for moving against the potential emotional impact for you and others in your family.

Pause, pray, cry, be truthful with yourself, ask for help, do your research, and walk into the next season, in the same home or a new home, one day at a time, by taking one step at a time.

Key points to consider:

- Give yourself time: Don't rush into major decisions like moving right after a loss; allow yourself time to process your emotions and grieve before making any significant changes.
- Evaluate your reasons: Is moving driven by a genuine need for a change, like a smaller space to manage, or is it an attempt to escape grief?

- Consult with support systems: Talk to close friends, family members, or a therapist about your feelings and whether moving might be beneficial for your situation.

- Consider the emotional impact: Moving can be stressful even under normal circumstances, so assess if you are emotionally ready to take on that additional burden while grieving.

- Think about the memories: If your current home is filled with strong memories of the deceased, moving could be a way to create a fresh start, but also consider if you're ready to let go of those memories.

- Practical considerations: Evaluate if the new space meets your needs, like accessibility, size, and proximity to support systems.

- Gradual changes: If you decide to move, consider making smaller changes to your current home first, like decluttering or redecorating, to ease into the transition.

Potential benefits of moving while grieving:

- Fresh start: A new environment could provide a sense of renewal and a chance to create new positive memories.

- Reduced triggers: If your current home is filled with reminders of the deceased, moving could help minimize triggering situations.

- Improved well-being: A change of scenery might contribute to a sense of personal agency and help the grieving process.

GOING BACK TO WORK + CHURCH

I was so blessed that I was given time to return to work after Jonathan passed away. There was never any pressure put on me to rush back. I have worked at my company for many years, and they were very good to me. I was off work for 3 weeks and started working at home for a few hours a day for the first week; catching up with everything that had hap-

CHAPTER 13

pened while I was out. The next week, I left the house and went into the stores again, and then a few days into that week, the world shut down because of covid-19. If you weren't around during the Coronavirus or don't remember that time, it was a once-in-a-lifetime experience. Everything was closed, and everyone was told to stay home; we were told that this would be for 2 weeks. This was very difficult for many and, at the same time, as scary as the unknown of the virus sweeping the nation and the world was. There was a collective sigh as everyone was given a moment to pause from the busyness of life.

Our family had been stopped in our tracks about a month prior and had already had to adjust to a new normal; we were experts at pivoting.

Now everything was different; there would be less missing Jonathan in the routines of our every day because we no longer had those routines. All the expectations of trying to carry on as usual, meet most deadlines, and mask any moments of overwhelming grief, were now gone.

Prior to this point, when I decided to go back to work, I was under the impression that my life and work responsibilities were continuing as normal. On my first day back, it was hard for me to focus, and I kept feeling like everything was the same in many ways, and maybe my home hadn't completely changed. As I saw my coworkers, they all told me that I shouldn't be at work and that I should be at home taking care of myself. I assured them that I was doing okay.

It helped that I didn't have to explain myself and why I had been out of work to people; many had kept up with my life via Facebook and had even attended the celebration of life for Jonathan. They had also been keeping up with the journal entries I had been sharing, so they had an inside view of my journey, which is not the common experience for most people walking through grief. I had also been in communication with stores to let them know I was returning, and they were very comforting and encouraging. So, it wasn't like I was encountering total strangers who I had to explain myself to or people I knew that weren't aware of what had happened in my life. Those seasons would come later, and I would have to decipher in those moments how to handle them.

Being able to stay home again was a blessing for me; there had been so many blessings along the way. Such as, If the world had "shutdown" 2 weeks earlier then no one would have been able to come to comfort us and be comforted because all flights were grounded and no one was allowed to gather in large groups. I would have felt very alone and there would be many people experiencing that loneliness in the coming months in 2020.

My company furloughed most of the field staff, and during that time, my family renovated a lot of our house. We did not own it, but the landlord was okay with all the renovations that we were doing. Our house had changed and so had we and everyone around us. We had all been through a shared trauma from the summer of 2020 and covid-19. Many people had lost loved ones, and we all knew that we were navigating and figuring out how to walk through this next season.

The 2nd time I returned to working in the stores, more time had passed. I was more comfortable with holding this grief that was traveling in life with me, and there was more of an outward focus on those around me that were hurting as well. This is how life is right—when you need comfort, others run to your side, and when others need comfort, you run to theirs, and that is how it should be.

While still at home, I joined a new church as well; this is where a lot more of the insecurity of identity came into play. How do you just open about something/someone so dear to your heart to complete strangers? A common question is, "How many children do you have?" when you meet someone, and each time I was faced with this question of how I would answer. Was it just a passing question, or was it someone who truly showed care and wanted to go below the surface? Sometimes, just saying, "I am here with my two girls," was truthful and enough information at that moment. And other times, in a more intimate setting, I would share that I also had a son, but he now was with Jesus in heaven. It's ok to tailor your answer; for me, it was always best to be as truthful as I could. And sometimes, as I shared about my girls publicly, I only cherished Jonathan in my heart, and that was ok, too.

I have also thought about how others carry details or experiences that they don't know how to share, so sometimes, I set an example for vulnerability. Showing that we are all in need of connection, and as you are navigating your own journey, you can give others the opportunity to comfort you, and you can also be an encouragement and comfort to others. When we share our struggles, we also have the opportunity to highlight the goodness of God. We have the opportunity to pray for one another so that the Lord will continue to sustain each one of us.

Returning to work after the death of your child can be challenging, but it's possible with the right support and realistic expectations.

You can try these tips:

- Take time off: Consider taking parental bereavement leave if it's available. You can also check with your employer about their bereavement leave policy.
- Communicate with your employer: Let your employer know how you're feeling and what support you need. You can discuss returning to work gradually, like working part-time or just in the mornings.
- Set manageable goals: Focus on short-term tasks and take breaks often throughout the day.
- Be realistic: Understand that grief can affect your job performance and satisfaction for a while.
- Practice self-care: Eat regularly, get enough sleep, and take walks in the fresh air.
- Accept that grief can last a long time: There's no set timeline for how long grief lasts, and it's okay to feel a range of emotions.

FINANCES

Financial stress in any season of life can be extremely challenging; then add to that the debilitating loss of your child that at times cripples your mind from the pain and shock. And now you must face a very expensive process of providing a final resting place for their body as well. It's not that you don't want to give your child, even at this point, all that you can, but sometimes there are just not enough financial resources to do so, or the costs could drain all that you have. So, what do you do in those situations?

If you have experienced losing your child then you have already had to face this, is your situation similar to mine or how did you handle those expenses? If you are in the position of not having experienced this great loss, it is important for us all to be as prepared as we can and encourage others to be as well. We should not be living in fear; but rather be wise with the resources the Lord has provided for us to steward.

First, you should research and may already have personal life insurance for your children to cover expenses. In our case, we had life insurance through my job. Unbeknownst to us until the moment that we needed it; Jonathan was the only member of the family who somehow had his policy canceled during open enrollment a few years prior.

It was listed in the overall breakdown that there were five policies in total, but in the portal, Jonathan was not selected as being covered. I tried to fight this with my company as I would not have made this change, and obviously there was a discrepancy. But they were unable to go back and retroactively correct this error. My advice is to ensure that during open enrollment, you double check the names covered. Since it is fresh on your mind right now, take the opportunity to check all the policies for your family.

This topic is not something that you want to think about or try to prepare for in case anything tragic happens. But it will relieve a lot of pressure, so limited finances do not add to an already stressful situation.

As we didn't have any help from insurance, my friend Jamie set up a GoFundMe account. Friends, family, and even strangers donated to help us cover expenses. There are a lot of people who are not able to be there for you in person or don't know what else to do or say. They would like to know that they are helping by donating any amount of money that they can.

There were many layers of needs during this time, and we shouldn't and couldn't ignore the real tangible needs. I think back to Jesus's ministry and how there were people who helped fund his ministry. They were vital to his ability to travel from town to town and buy food for himself and his disciples.

Because of that funding, he was able to travel there and heal and share the Gospel with all who would listen. I guess what I am getting at is not to feel bad by letting people know there is a need. They want to contribute to your family, your closure and your healing. It is their way of being the hands and feet of Jesus. It is a blessing for them to give and for you to receive.

If you still have a need, then looking at your own savings or investments may be necessary. Again, this is the last thing that you want to dip into your savings or gains from investment for, but you must do what is needed in these very difficult situations.

Do not let it become an area of stress, worry, and regret for you. Release all expenses and how they will be or were paid for. Know that you did your best with what was in your hands and the great weight on your shoulders.

Key options to consider:

- Life insurance: Check if the deceased child has a life insurance policy, particularly a "final expense" policy designed specifically for funeral costs.
- Employer benefits: Some employers may offer survivor benefits that can contribute towards funeral expenses.
- Child bereavement charities: Organizations like "The TEARS Foundation" or "Child Funeral Charity" provide financial assistance to families dealing with the loss of a child.
- Crowdfunding: Platforms like GoFundMe allow you to create a campaign to raise funds from friends, family, and the community.
- Child's personal accounts: If the deceased child had a Uniform Gift to Minors Act (UGMA) or Uniform Transfer to Minors Act (UTMA) account, these funds may be accessible to cover funeral costs.
- Government assistance: Depending on your location, there might be government programs offering limited financial support for the funeral expenses.

CLOSING LETTER

"The lord is my shepherd; I shall not want. He makes me lie down in green pastures. He leads me beside still waters. He restores my soul. He leads me in paths of righteousness for his name's sake. Even though I walk through the valley of the shadow of death, I will fear no evil, for you are with me; your rod and your staff, they comfort me. you prepare a table before me in the presence of my enemies; you anoint my head with oil; my cup overflows. Surely goodness and mercy shall follow me all the days of my life, and I shall dwell in the house of the lord forever." Psalm 23

In closing, I want to leave this Psalm with you; it is a great depiction of the journey we walk through in life. Times of celebration and abundance, and times of walking through the valley of the shadow of death.

The first thing that the Lord establishes is His relationship with us, He is our foundation through every season. He is our shepherd, our provider, and our protector. He is invested in every area of our lives, and we can trust Him to provide for every need; we shall not want. He provides rest for our weary souls (He makes me lie down in green pastures) and refreshment as we walk by and drink from the still waters.

There's a reason why before we walk through the valley (testing and trials), the Lord gives us promises of His rest, refreshment, healing (He restores my soul), guidance (he leads me in the paths of righteousness) and purpose (for his name's sake).

He reassures us before we need that reassurance because He knows we are prone to fear and to doubt His protection and faithfulness. He assures us that His faithful rod and staff will corral us back into alignment if we stray and keep us from danger, as a loving shepherd and father does.

He reminds us that He has defeated the enemy, and we are protected from ultimate defeat; we can trust in His finished work. He consecrates us and anoints us for the journey ahead.

My cup runneth over—this part is hard to take hold of and believe in our present circumstance, do we truly believe that we have all we need in Christ to overflowing. I think when we consider that without Him that we have nothing, we realize that with Him we have everything—to overflowing.

We can be confident in the goodness of the Lord, that His intentions and motivations are always good. His mercy that welcomes us into His loving arms, is available to us each and every morning. We have been welcomed into His house, His family, His inheritance forever for all eternity. We can be confident that the pain of this world will not last forever, but the joy of our salvation surely will. Amen

Our HOPE is in Him. We do not grieve as the world does without Hope. 1 Thessalonians 4:13

Recently, I was listening to the book by Elisabeth Elliot, Suffering Is Never for Nothing. She talks about how God invited her into glorifying Him and releasing to Him, what He had placed in her hands. In every situation He is inviting each of us to release everything to Him as well.

Will you release the loss of your child to Him? When you release it, you no longer need to figure it out or justify it with cliches. Releasing it takes the weight off of your shoulders and invites Him to bring healing, purpose, and redemption to every pain and loss. He will forge us in and by the fire and fortify us for the road ahead.

CLOSING LETTER

Friends, thank you for taking this journey with me thus far. I invite you to reach out to me so we can continue to support each other in seasons of celebration and mourning. I would love for our conversation to continue in our Celebrate and Inspire Life Collective Facebook group, a collection of women sharing our stories and finding joy in seeking the Lord in every season. We have the opportunity to glorify the Lord together, remind each other of His goodness, and find strength in a community of like-minded believers.

I have also provided a qr code below that you can scan for a list of resources I have referenced in this book and others that have been a great support to me, including a Spotify music playlist. You can access my newsletter through this qr code as well.

Lastly, REVIEWS! If the Lord has ministered to you through this book and you would like to help others discover it, your review helps immensely. You can leave a review on Amazon, Goodreads or other platforms. On Amazon, go to the book page, scroll to the bottom of the page until you see "Write a Review." You just write your name, a title for the review, and the review itself. That's it. The whole process takes about 5-10 minutes. I would be so grateful.

Until next time,

May the Lord bless you and keep you; the Lord make His face shine upon you, And be gracious to you; The Lord lift up His countenance upon you, And give you peace. Numbers 6:22-26

Instagram: @deborah_simpson1
Facebook: Celebrate and Inspire Life Collective
Email: deborah@celebrateandinspirelife.com
Website: celebrateandinspirelife.com
QR: https://celebrateandinspirelife.myflodesk.com/connect

ACKNOWLEDGMENTS

Mom, I know that my strength comes fully from the Lord, but I also know that strength has been passed down from you. When I lost Jonathan, I got a glimpse of the loss you felt when dad died, except your different burden to bear was raising us 3 children alone. Thank you for all the seeds of prayer that you have sown in private and public. Thank you for running to my side as soon as you heard the news and for staying to care for me, to ensure I pulled myself out of all the questioning and despair; and to make sure I ate something nutritious and healthy every day. You walked through each step of those initial weeks with me, and I couldn't have done it without you. You have been a loving, present mother and Granmax and a faithful friend.

Rachel, the ways that you have added to my life and helped to hold me up are countless; thank you would never be enough. Your selfless, generous heart is your best quality; it has been a privilege being your sister. I marvel at how intentional you are to be in my life and my children's life. This book would not have come to fruition without you in so many ways. I know that I can always ask you about a myriad of topics and get an answer full of wisdom, a deep thought process and an imagination beyond compare. I hope you know how loved you are by all who encounter you and that you find rest in Him.

Grandma, you have passed down to us your love of taking family pictures and because of this, we have many pictures of memories to look back on of Jonathan and reminisce about. Thank you for always being a prayer warrior in our family and for stepping in physically from when I was a child and with my children. Even so much as to take care of Jonathan when he was just a newborn, that was a difficult season for all involved but a time we both cherish. I have loved deepening our relationship in the last few years and look forward to many more times together.

Simon, we have been through a lot as siblings over the past 5 years, I treasure how our relationship has deepened. Being very similar in personalities we get each other but often in the past, the words would escape us and be left unsaid. Know that I value you as a godly, mighty man in our family and you are needed and vital.

Adam, thank you for the time and attention you always gave Jonathan, I know that sitting in your plane was a highlight of his last trip to Ohio. I value the friendship and support you have always shown me. I enjoy our discussions about business, politics or different treatments we were looking into.

Anthony, we may be walking different paths now but thank you for how you kept our family going after Jonathan's passing. I know that you were struggling yourself, but you showed what a true husband and father is like during trials, both tender and a strong protector. Our children are blessed to have you in their lives.

Uncle David + Auntie Susan, since I was a child, your family has been a refuge from the storm. I still remember the providential day that we met; the Lord continues to weave our families together as my children enjoy growing with your grandchildren. Thank you for always making an effort to be present for the celebrations and the times of mourning. You have carried the mantle of father to not only your own children, but me and my siblings as well.

Beatriz, thank you for the immense amount of joy you have brought to my life and our whole family over the years of being, The Neighbors. My girls will always think about the long days of playing that turned into movie nights and sleepovers and pancake breakfasts. Our impulse girls' outings are always the best, just when we don't think things will work out, they turn out perfect. There were many times that you pulled me out into the sun after Jonathan's passing, in my robe and all. You have been my go-to for so many things and always listen to my crazy new venture and support me however you can. You are a true friend to so many and I am blessed to be loved by you.

Natalie, as long as I have been in Miami you have been in my life, we have grown together and been there for celebrations and the hardest parts of each other's lives. Who would have thought that when I hired you in Coconut Grove that I would be living in your apartment all these years later and our girls would be friends since they were babies. Thank you for always being willing to drop everything and come to my side. I wouldn't have made it through many seasons without you reading my

ACKNOWLEDGEMENTS

epistles via text messages and responding. I gave you a break by writing this book. Lol

Kristina, I love how you are intentional about keeping up traditions and we know that we have each other's back. Thank you for not pulling away when the pain of your own loss may have been too much to be there for me. You loved Jonathan as your own and stepped in right away to make his bookmark, get balloons and cater for Jonathan's celebration of life. You have flourished as a mom to baby Javi, and it brings me so much joy to see you happy. We will always remember our girls' first argument in pre k and how they ended up best friends from it.

Jesus + Blanca, you have always been mentors that I have looked up to and have had the privilege over the years to call you friends and now pastors. Thank you for the devotion to the Lord, your family and to service that you display. How you showed up in countless ways after Jonathan's passing, from offering comfort to helping to organize at the funeral home, to making our Simpson t-shirts, that I was just baptized in for consecration recently. You both have been a voice of wisdom and a shoulder to cry on through so many seasons and you throw a great party too.

Christina, thank you for jumping in and listening to my heart and honoring my specific wishes for Jonathan's celebration of life. I always cherish when memories come up of when we first met at crew. You have modeled how to care for and intentionality pour into people in your life; I am blessed to be a recipient.

Jamie, thank you for how you have always had an open door and a willing heart to scoop everybody up, feed them, dress them and show them a good time. For how you welcomed Alayna into the hospital and all you helped organize to support our family monetarily and logistically with the funeral home. You have been a faithful friend and an example to me of how to enjoy life to the fullest.

Brittany, from twin geo metros in college to walking through the last 22 years together. You have shown me how to physically stay part of someone's life even when you live across the country...I'm sure the fact that I live where you want to vacation has nothing to do with it. You have been a voice of wisdom, faith, sound doctrine and a constant friend to always lean on. Your thoughtfulness to always send packages for me and the girls and speak life into them is priceless and I know you constantly hold us up in prayer. You have been vital in the release of this book; thank you for all your input.

Cari, the moment our girls met was truly orchestrated by the Lord; he knew that you would be exactly what Katie needed in the weeks following Jonathan's passing. You have been a tower of strength and a cheerleader always in my corner. I treasure the times when you call me to pray for you or your kids, I love having that connection and celebrating our girls growing in their faith. To many more years of our friendship and our girls' friendship growing.

Martha, you are mother and grandmother to countless and it is an honor to call you friend and mentor. Thank you for how you have shown up in my life cheering me on and speaking life into me. You are an example of living a life of service and devotion to God and it is my privilege to play a small part in your mission at Heartbeat. I knew right away that I wanted you to write the foreword for my book, our hearts and words are now connected forever.

Maggy, I still remember when Annette told me her aunt taught piano and gave me your number and the rest is history. You have always been more than a piano teacher. Friend, counselor, confidant, and cheerleader to name a few. Thank you for checking in and paying attention to what I post and talk about, I can always count on having a meaningful conversation with you.

Yamila, the way that the Lord brought us together as we were both visiting the cemetery is a story I will always cherish. An unfortunate situation for us both but a friendship that has been so lifegiving. A testament to how the Lord redeems and brings beauty from ashes. Thank you for always encouraging me to step outside my comfort zone and being up for anything at a moment's notice. It was my pleasure co leading the Foster Respite Ministry and seeing the Lord move with our small yes, both in our hearts and theirs.

Robert, unbeknownst to me, there were many years that you admired Jesus in me, from afar. Thank you for the endless encouragement you give and the way you celebrate the gifts and talents the Lord has placed in me. You provide a listening ear and a sounding board for me to voice my ideas and help me navigate making decisions, often without saying a word. You have been an example to me of how to love others and live a life of service to the Lord; continuously listening to His voice.

Vous, thank you for being by our side from very early that morning; Pastor Dawn Chere, Crew Leaders and members, Kids Ministry lead and others. You welcomed us back with open arms and made us feel loved and supported and cared for. You have walked through many seasons with us, before and after Jonathan's passing.

Trinity, thank you for being an extension of Vous and making Jonathan's celebration of life everything we wanted it to be. Pastor Rich sr. for encouraging Anthony to run to the Lord and not away from Him in his greatest time of devastation.

PRC, you genuinely were eager to welcome us into your church family. Providing a safe place for me to share a sacred part of my life with those who hadn't walked through it with me and didn't know Jonathan. You taught me how to respond in a compassionate way and walk alongside each other. You deepened my love and depth of knowledge of the theology of the Christian life and solidified seeing Jesus revealed in all of scripture. Thank you for walking with me through the 2nd hardest season of my life, transitioning from married to divorced. You have been a voice of wisdom, a shoulder to cry on, constant prayer, support and an example to my girls of godly, selfless men who serve with excellence and a willing spirit.

LH Ekklesia, thank you for expanding my vision of the global church and living in the Kingdom now. For being a conduit of the Lord's healing and freedom from the trauma and wounds that were manifesting in my life. This book would not exist if you had not believed in my purpose and held me accountable to make a goal and stick to it. You showed me how I was the Lord's beloved and I will forever cherish the moment I felt His love completely surround and fill me.

One Name, I only started attending in May 2024, but our hearts were always connected. Thank you for welcoming me in when I would stop by sporadically to support you in the early days. It has been such an encouragement to me to see your growth and depth as a church. Thank you, ladies, of ONC for seeing me and seeing the strength the Lord has placed in me. For always encouraging me, caring for me and praying for me. For showing me what it means to be led by the spirit and welcoming the

Lord into every area of your life. You have been an example of living out of our identity in Christ as sons and daughters and living in freedom.

Guess Family, thank you for the care, grace and understanding shown during the hardest season of my life. It is not common for a workplace to display those characteristics; I know that it's the special people I have been blessed to work with for over the last 20 years who make all the difference.

My Online Community, there are so many of you who have joined me and supported me on my journey, whether you are a childhood friend or family who love from afar. Or maybe we have never met in person, but we feel like best friends through the screen, as our hearts are united together, so thank you. It is an honor to be welcomed into your life and for you to choose to be a part of mine. The ability to see how the Lord speaks to your heart through my words and speaks to my heart through yours, is such a gift.

ABOUT THE AUTHOR

Born in a bamboo hut built by her father in the hills of Jamaica, Deborah Simpson is a woman forged by both fire and faith. She spent her childhood in Montego Bay, where her earliest memories were filled with love, and the beauty of island life. After the heartbreaking loss of her father at age seven, she was raised by a praying single mother who laid the foundation for the woman of faith she would become. That legacy of strength has carried Deborah through a life filled with both extraordinary highs and heartbreaking lows.

Deborah is the proud mother of three children— two daughters in college and her beloved son in heaven. She's walked through unexpected seasons in motherhood, marriage, and divorce, all while clinging to the unshakeable hope she found in Jesus.

Her personal journey of grief and healing has become the heartbeat of her life's work: inspiring women to trust God in every season and to find purpose in the pain. Now living in Miami, Florida for over 20 years, Deborah is the founder of Celebrate + Inspire Life(.com) and the voice behind the Celebrate + Inspire Life Podcast, a growing community and platform dedicated to helping women to worship and surrender through every season with purpose and joy.

What started as a God-given vision has become a mission field— equipping women to live joyfully, serve faithfully, and never lose sight of God's hand, even in life's darkest moments.

With over 24 years in the retail industry, Deborah understands the rhythm of balancing career, motherhood, ministry, and personal growth.

She's also pursued several side businesses over the years, not just for financial freedom, but to connect deeply with others and walk in obedience to what God places on her heart.

She is currently expanding Celebrate + Inspire Life into an online ministry platform offering devotionals, resources, and events designed to support women walking through grief, transition, and spiritual transformation.

Deborah holds a Bachelor of Science in Small Business Management and Entrepreneurship. She's also a graduate of the LH Kingdom Leadership Academy and the Virtual Assistant Internship, blending her entrepreneurial spirit with her heart for service. Whether she's donating time and resources to ministries like Heartbeat of Miami, serving foster families through with her church, or supporting moms in crisis through Safe Families of Miami, Deborah is committed to being the hands and feet of Jesus wherever He leads her.

Through every triumph and trial, Deborah's desire remains the same: to glorify God, inspire women to seek Him above all else, and leave a legacy of faith, service, and love.

Her story is a testament to what happens when you trust God with the broken pieces—and allow Him to write a story that brings Him all the glory and you into your purpose.